D0923438

PROPERTY OF
TRINIDAD HIGH
SCHOOL LIBRARY

Date Due

NOV 25			
MAY 23 '75			
MAY 15 '76			
MAR 11 '80			
MAR 4 '86			

Demco 293-5

Times Three

ALSO BY PHYLLIS McGINLEY

VERSE
On the Contrary
One More Manhattan
Pocketful of Wry
Husbands Are Difficult
Stones from a Glass House
A Short Walk from the Station
The Love Letters of Phyllis McGinley
Merry Christmas, Happy New Year

PROSE
The Province of the Heart

PHYLLIS McGINLEY

Times Three

SELECTED VERSE FROM THREE DECADES

WITH SEVENTY NEW POEMS

FOREWORD BY W. H. AUDEN

NEW YORK   THE VIKING PRESS   1961

PROPERTY OF
TRINIDAD HIGH
SCHOOL LIBRARY

Copyright © each year 1932–1960 by Phyllis McGinley

Published in 1960 by The Viking Press, Inc.
625 Madison Avenue, New York 22, N.Y.

Published simultaneously in Canada by
The Macmillan Company of Canada Limited

Fourth printing May 1961

Many of the poems in this collection were first published in *The New Yorker*, others in *America, The
American Scholar, The Atlantic, The Common-
weal, Cosmopolitan, Forum, Good Housekeeping,
The Griffin, Harper's Bazaar, Harper's Magazine,
Mademoiselle, The New York American, New
York Herald Tribune, The New York Times, Saturday Review, Woman's Day, Ladies Home Journal* and *The Saturday Evening Post*. Copyright ©
1938–1942, 1944, 1945, 1958, 1959 by The Curtis
Publishing Company.

Library of Congress catalog card number: 60–11011

DESIGNED BY JANET HALVERSON

Printed in the United States of America
W

For Charles, Julie and Pat,
my critics, my champions, my copy

CONTENTS

FOREWORD

by W. H. Auden

Phyllis McGinley needs no puff. Her poems are known and loved by tens of thousands. They call for no learned exegesis. If a Ph.D. thesis is ever written about her work, it will be in an alien tongue and an alien alphabet.

I start a sentence: "The poetry of Phyllis McGinley is . . . ," and there I stick, for all I wish to say is ". . . is the poetry of Phyllis McGinley," a statement which I can prove to be true by quoting at random.

> . . . By day the chattering mowers cope
> With grass decreed a final winner.
> Darkness delays. The skipping rope
> Twirls in the driveway after dinner.
>
> Through lupine-lighted borders now
> For winter bones Dalmatians forage.
> Costly the spray on apple bough.
> The canvas chair comes out of storage;
>
> And rose-red golfers dream of par,
> And class-bound children loathe their labors,
> While pilgrims, touring gardens, are
> Cold to petunias of their neighbors. . . .

Without knowing who wrote them, I could recognize the genre of English poetry to which such lines belong, and name some of the masters in it—Hood, Praed, Calverley, Belloc, Chesterton. But when, instead of looking at their style and technique, I think of writers with a comparable kind of sensibility, a similar cast of

ix

imagination, the names that come to mind have either, like Jane Austen, Colette, and Virginia Woolf, written in prose, or, like Laura Riding and Marianne Moore, written poetry in a totally different style. What, in fact, distinguishes Phyllis McGinley's poems from those of most light-verse poets is that no man could have written them. The masculine and feminine imagination are not mutually exclusive—the hundred-per-cent male and the hundred-per-cent female are equally insufferable—but they can, I believe, be differentiated. There are two questions about which it seems to me fascinating to speculate: firstly, "What does the poetry men write owe to the influence of women, whether as mothers, sisters, and wives, or as women authors whom they admire?" and secondly, "What can women who write learn from men and what should they beware of imitating in masculine literature?"

Naturally, I first look to see what Phyllis McGinley has to say on these matters. She speaks up bravely for her own sex.

> *For the female of the species may be deadlier than the male*
> *But she can make herself a cup of coffee without reducing*
> *The entire kitchen to a shambles.*

> Perverse though their taste in cravats
>   Is deemed by their lords and their betters,
> They know the importance of hats
>   And they write you the news in their letters.
> Their minds may be lighter than foam,
>   Or altered in haste and in hurry,
> But they seldom bring company home
>   When you're warming up yesterday's curry.

> *And when lovely woman stoops to folly,*
> *She does not invariably come in at four A.M.,*
> *Singing "Sweet Adeline."*

On the other hand, she is no ferocious feminist; she is willing to admit that we have a few small virtues.

> For invitations you decry
> He furnisheth an alibi.
> He jousts with taxi-men in tourney,
> He guards your luggage when you journey,

And brings you news and quotes you facts
And figures out your income tax
And slaughters spiders when you daren't
And makes a very handy parent.

But, of course, from the beginning, little boys can never hope to be as smart as little girls. Compare their reactions when they can no longer believe in Santa Claus.

For little boys are rancorous
When robbed of any myth,
And spiteful and cantankerous
To all their kin and kith.
But little girls can draw conclusions
And profit from their lost illusions.

The masculine imagination lives in a state of perpetual revolt against the limitations of human life. In theological terms, one might say that all men, left to themselves, become gnostics. They may swagger like peacocks, but in their heart of hearts they all think sex an indignity and wish they could beget themselves on themselves. Hence the aggressive hostility toward women so manifest in most club-car stories.

Hence also their attitude toward matter: they love chopping and sawing and drilling and hammering, and it gives them as much pleasure, perhaps even more, to knock a building down as to put one up. And when matter rebels against their injustice, when collar studs roll away and umbrellas go into hiding, they are helpless and have to cry for rescue to their wives.

Left to itself the masculine imagination has very little appreciation for the here and now; it prefers to dwell on what is absent, on what has been or may be. If men are more punctual than women, it is because they know that, without the external discipline of clock time, they would never get anything done.

Above all, the masculine imagination is essentially theatrical. In comparison with women, men are poor liars because their sense of the difference between fact and fiction is so much vaguer: even in domestic life a man expects to be admired, not for telling the truth, but for telling a good story well. Among the poets, the purest examples of the masculine imagination that I know are Victor Hugo and W. B. Yeats. Who could possibly conceive of either of them as a woman?

In contrast, the feminine imagination accepts facts and is coolly realistic. There are certain resemblances between the lines from "June in the Suburbs" which I quoted on page ix and the poetry of John Betjeman, but what makes it impossible that Mr. Betjeman could have written them is their total lack of nostalgia. A striking illustration of this is a "sad" poem, "Blues for a Melodion." The theme of this, the passing of youth and the oncome of middle-age, has frequently been treated by men. As a rule, they devote their words to their memories of themselves—once I could run very fast, once I was much admired by the girls, once I was very bright, etc., but now . . . In Phyllis McGinley's poem, the "I" does not appear until the last two lines and the past is hardly mentioned.

A castor's loose on the buttoned chair—
  The one upholstered in shabby coral.
I never noticed, before, that tear
  In the dining-room paper.

When did the rocker cease to rock,
  The fringe sag down on the corner sofa?
All of a sudden the Meissen clock
  Has a cherub missing.

All of a sudden the plaster chips,
  The carpet frays by the morning windows;
Careless, a rod from the curtain slips,
  And the gilt is tarnished.

This is the house that I knew by heart.
  Everything here seemed sound, immortal.
When did this delicate ruin start?
  How did the moth come?

Naked by daylight, the paint is airing
  Its rags and tatters. There's dust on the mantel.
And who is that gray-haired stranger staring
  Out of my mirror?

So, too, in her satirical pieces. Confronted with things and people who do not please her, she does not, like many male satirists, lose her temper or even show shocked surprise; she merely observes what is the case with deadly accuracy.

Evening Musicale

Candles. Red tulips, ninety cents the bunch.
  Two lions, Grade B. A newly tuned piano.
No cocktails, but a dubious kind of punch,
  Lukewarm and weak. A harp and a soprano.
The "Lullaby" of Brahms. Somebody's cousin
  From Forest Hills, addicted to the pun.
Two dozen gentlemen; ladies, three dozen,
  Earringed and powdered. Sandwiches at one.

The ash trays few, the ventilation meager.
Shushes to greet the late-arriving guest
Or quell the punch-bowl group. A young man eager
To render "Danny Deever" by request.
And sixty people trying to relax
On little rented chairs with gilded backs.

After reading this, anyone who, like myself, has had the honor of entertaining Phyllis McGinley, will think twice about inviting her again.

Women do not, I think, excel at what is conventionally called Love Poetry. Indeed, when they try, the results can be embarrassingly awful—think of poor Mrs. Browning. Perhaps the feminine imagination is too serious. Men can write good love poems because they are always aware that the girl they happen to be in love with might be someone else (and often one suspects that they are thinking of several girls at the same time). But women write better than men about marriage. When a husband does write about his wife, which is rare, he is apt to become weepy. Not so a wife writing about a husband.

In garden-colored boots he goes
  Ardent around perennial borders
To spray the pink, celestial rose
  Or give a weed its marching orders.

> Draining at dawn his hasty cup,
>   He takes a train to urban places;
> By lamplight, cheerful, figures up
>   The cost of camps and dental braces.
>
> And warm upon my shoulders lays
>   Impetuous at dinner table
> The mantle of familiar praise
>   That's better than a coat of sable.

In order to write well about children, it would seem that a man must be, like Lewis Carroll or Hans Andersen, a bachelor, but a woman a mother. When fathers write about their offspring, their chief concern is not the child as child but the future adult they hope or fear it will grow into. Bachelors, with their masculine nostalgia for their own childhood, are better than women, perhaps, at understanding the fantasy life of children, but only a mother can convey a sense of their physical presence.

> Oh, the peace like heaven
>   That wraps me around,
> Say, at eight-thirty-seven,
>   When they're schoolroom-bound
> With the last glove mated
>   And the last scarf tied,
> With the pig-tail plaited,
>   With the pincurl dried,
> And the egg disparaged
>   And the porridge sneered at,
> And last night's comics furtively peered at,
> The coat apprehended
>   On its ultimate hook,
> And the cover mended
>   On the history book!

There is, perhaps, one thing which women can profitably learn from men, a sense of play. Left to itself, the feminine imagination would get so serious that it would look down on the arts as unworthy frivolities. Phyllis McGinley has her fair element of masculine imagination, to which she owes, among other things, her dexterity in rhyming. But she does not go in for ostentatiously farcical rhymes like

> Among the anthropophagi
> One's friends are one's sarcophagi
> > (Ogden Nash)

or puns like

> The bar-maid of the Crown he lov'd,
> From whom he never ranged,
> For though he changed his horses there,
> His love he never changed.

> He thought her fairest of all fares,
> So fondly love prefers;
> And often, among twelve outsides,
> Deem'd no outside like hers.
> > (Thomas Hood)

I think she is wise to avoid such things. A gift for standing on one's head and pulling faces seems to be a masculine gift. There have been wonderful comediennes, but who has heard of a woman clown?

Clowns are enchanting in their proper place, the stage, but in real life, private or public, they can be boring and a menace. Ten minutes with a newspaper leave me with the conviction that the human race has little chance of survival unless men are disenfranchised and debarred from political life: in a technological age, only women have the sense to know which toys are dangerous.

> Let them on Archimedes dote
> Who like to hear the planet rattling.
> I cannot cast a hearty vote
> For Galileo or for Gatling,
> Preferring, of the Freaks of science,
> The pygmies rather than the giants—

> (*And from experience being wary of
> Greek geniuses bearing gifts*)—

Deciding on reflection calm,
    Mankind is better off with trifles:
With Band-Aid rather than the bomb,
    With safety match than safety rifles.
Let the earth fall or the earth spin!
A brave new world might well begin
With no invention
Worth the mention
Save paper towels and aspirin.

As for the arts, it may be true that up till now the greatest artists have been men, but from whom did they get the notion of making anything in the first place? Their motive is implied in Dr. Johnson's reply to the lady who asked him to define the difference between men and women: "I can't conceive, Madam, can you?"

The Fifties

A LITTLE NIGHT MUSIC

The Conquerors

It seems vainglorious and proud
Of Atom-man to boast aloud
   His prowess homicidal
When one remembers how for years,
With their rude stones and humble spears,
Our sires, at wiping out their peers,
   Were almost never idle.

Despite his under-fissioned art
The Hittite made a splendid start
   Toward smiting lesser nations;
While Tamerlane, it's widely known,
Without a bomb to call his own
   Destroyed whole populations.

Nor did the ancient Persian need
Uranium to kill his Mede,
   The Viking earl, his foeman.
The Greeks got excellent results
With swords and engined catapults.
   A chariot served the Roman.

Mere cannon garnered quite a yield
On Waterloo's tempestuous field.
   At Hastings and at Flodden

Stout countrymen, with just a bow
And arrow, laid their thousands low.
      And Gettysburg was sodden.

Though doubtless now our shrewd machines
Can blow the world to smithereens
      More tidily and so on,
Let's give our ancestors their due.
Their ways were coarse, their weapons few.
But ah! how wondrously they slew
      With what they had to go on.

The Day After Sunday

Always on Monday, God's in the morning papers,
   His Name is a headline, His Works are rumored abroad.
Having been praised by men who are movers and shapers,
   From prominent Sunday pulpits, newsworthy is God.

On page 27, just opposite Fashion Trends,
   One reads at a glance how He scolded the Baptists a little,
Was firm with the Catholics, practical with the Friends,
   To Unitarians pleasantly noncommittal.

In print are His numerous aspects, too: God smiling,
   God vexed, God thunderous, God whose mansions are pearl,
Political God, God frugal, God reconciling
   Himself with science, God guiding the Camp Fire Girl.

Always on Monday morning the press reports
   God as revealed to His vicars in various guises—
Benevolent, stormy, patient, or out of sorts.
   God knows which God is the God God recognizes.

Reflections at Dawn

I wish I owned a Dior dress
   Made to my order out of satin.
I wish I weighed a little less
   And could read Latin,
Had perfect pitch or matching pearls,
   A better head for street directions,
And seven daughters, all with curls
   And fair complexions.
I wish I'd tan instead of burn.
   But most, on all the stars that glisten,
I wish at parties I could learn
   To sit and listen.

I wish I didn't talk so much at parties.
It isn't that I want to hear
My voice assaulting every ear,
Uprising loud and firm and clear
   Above the cocktail clatter.
It's simply, once a doorbell's rung,
(I've been like this since I was young)
Some madness overtakes my tongue
   And I begin to chatter.

Buffet, ball, banquet, quilting bee,
   Wherever conversation's flowing,
Why must I feel it falls on me
   To keep things going?
Though ladies cleverer than I
   Can loll in silence, soft and idle,
Whatever topic gallops by,
   I seize its bridle,
Hold forth on art, dissect the stage,
   Or babble like a kindergart'ner
Of politics till I enrage
   My dinner partner.

I wish I didn't talk so much at parties.
When hotly boil the arguments,

Ah! would I had the common sense
To sit demurely on a fence
  And let who will be vocal,
Instead of plunging in the fray
With my opinions on display
Till all the gentlemen edge away
  To catch an early local.

Oh! there is many a likely boon
  That fate might flip me from her griddle.
I wish that I could sleep till noon
  And play the fiddle,
Or dance a *tour jeté* so light
  It would not shake a single straw down.
But when I ponder how last night
  I laid the law down,
More than to have the Midas touch
  Or critics' praise, however hearty,
I wish I didn't talk so much,
I wish I didn't talk so much,
I wish I didn't talk so much
  When I am at a party.

Rock-'n'-Roll Session

For this the primal reed was cloven.
For this did Berlioz break his ease
And Schubert starve and deaf Beethoven
Bend silence into symphonies.

For this the little Mozart fiddled
Beyond his bedtime, Bach was born,
And Guido got the scale unriddled:
That, paced by an hysteric horn,

The pimpled heirs of Orpheus, beating
Damp palms, might sway (agape like fish)
To four notes endlessly repeating
Thirty-two bars of gibberish.

A Threnody

"The new Rolls-Royce is designed to be owner driven. *No chauffeur*
required."   —*From an advertisement in* **The New Yorker.**

Grandeur, farewell.
Farewell, pomp, glory, wealth's indulgent voice.
Tyre turned to dust in time. Great Carthage fell.
And owner-driven is the new Rolls-Royce.

Behold it, democratic front to back;
Nimble when traffic pinches;
Steered, braked by power; briefer than Cadillac
By eighteen inches;
Humming at sixty with an eerie purr
But needing no chauffeur.

What does it signify if radiator
(Altered but once, and that in '33,
When, at Sir Henry's death, or a little later,
The red R R was re-
Placed by a less conspicuous ebony)
Keeps still its ancient shape? What matter whether
The seats no minion now will ever use
Come padded in eight hides of English leather—
Enough for one hundred and twenty-eight pairs of shoes?
That the paint glistens and the brasses shine
More lusterful than hope?
That engineers have listened for axle-whine
With a stethoscope?

Splendor decays, despite the walnut table
Sliding from under the dash. Who now will stow
The wicker hampers away? For ladies in sable,
Who'll spread the cloth, uncork the Veuve Clicquot?
Who'll clean
The optional-special espresso coffee machine,

From folding bed whip off the cover of baize, or
Guard the electric razor?

Who but the owner-driver, squinting ahead
Through the marvelous glass, fretting when lights are red,
Studying on his lap
The cryptic, cross-marked, wife-defeating map?
He, it is he,
Tooling toward Cambridge, say (or Yale or Colgate),
On football afternoons, must nervously
Fumble for change at the tollgate,
Curse the careering drivers of both genders
Whose rods are hot,
Fear for his fourteen-times-enameled fenders,
Search out the parking lot,
Remember the chains of winter, wrench the round wheel
Against the arrogant trucks, nor ever feel
Less mortal than man in Minx or Oldsmobile.

No one remains to touch a decorous forelock
Or fold a monogrammed blanket over the knees.
Gone the chauffeur—gone like Merlin the Warlock
And the unmourned chemise.
Gone newsboy's Grail, all that is rich and choice
And suave as David Niven.
Grandeur, a long farewell. The new Rolls-Royce
Is owner-driven.

My Six Toothbrushes

Against the pure, reflective tiles,
Northeast a little of the shower,
Gaudy as crocuses they flower.

The colors vary; but the styles
Are recommended and didactic
(Some Fuller and some Prophylactic.)

I cannot, it is strange, recall
When impulse sent me forth to buy
These gauds, or where or even why.

But here they dangle on my wall,
Symbols of vanity and hope.
I watch them shimmer while I soap

And am astonished, more or less,
Discovering how has lived in me
Such rage against mortality

That I this morning should possess
Six, six! and all set dense as thistles
With tough, imperishable bristles.

Polychromatic, they confront
My startled, half-abluted eyes.
Do these, I think, epitomize

The frivolous trophies of my Hunt?
Is my one Creed, my guidestar polar,
In corpore sano, sana molar,

Which has no care for kind or witty
Or learned ways or actual grace?
Disturbing. Well, in any case,

At least they do look rather pretty
Hanging redundantly in files
Against the cool, reflective tiles.

The Landscape of Love

I

Do not believe them. Do not believe what strangers
Or casual tourists, moored a night and day
In some snug, sunny, April-sheltering bay
(Along the coast and guarded from great dangers)
Tattle to friends when ignorant they return.
Love is no lotus-island endlessly
Washed by a summer ocean, no Capri;
But a huge landscape, perilous and stern—

More poplared than the nations to the north,
More bird-beguiled, stream-haunted. But the ground
Shakes underfoot. Incessant thunders sound,
Winds shake the trees, and tides run back and forth
And tempests winter there, and flood and frost
In which too many a voyager is lost.

II

None knows this country save the colonist,
His homestead planted. He alone has seen
The hidden groves unconquerably green,
The secret mountains steepling through the mist.
Each is his own discovery. No chart
Has pointed him past chasm, bog, quicksand,
Earthquake, mirage, into his chosen land—
Only the steadfast compass of the heart.

Turn a deaf ear, then, on the traveler who,
Speaking a foreign tongue, has never stood
Upon love's hills or in a holy wood
Sung incantations; yet, having bought a few
Postcards and trinkets at some cheap bazaar,
Cries, "This and thus the God's dominions are!"

Against Hope

When mischievous Pandora (the first woman),
Greedy for what was hid
In Jove's great box, succumbed to being human
And flipped, as it were, her lid,
All miseries, they say, went pouring past her
Into the world's scope—
Every conceivable ill, plague, spite, disaster.
But at the end came Hope,
A fluttering envoy always in reach, on call.
And Hope was worst of all.

Alas, Pandora! Had she only been
Quicker to act or else more dilatory
And trapped the insect in,
Our chroniclers could tell a different story.
Man, the poor beast,
Might have become accustomed to life's uses,
Put up with famine nor awaited feast,
Accepted his bruises,
His lumps and bumps and smarts and his crops of stone.
But Hope never lets him alone.

Louder than famished midges, buzzing and humming,
Hope swarms at his shoulder, makes him promises of
Goals, grails, importances, a Second Coming,
Unnotional love,
No later than Tuesday. He cannot sit down in tears
But Hope whines round his ears
All lies and tattle.

"That cloud," she whispers, "from which has lately come
Lightning to take your homestead and your cattle,
Look! may be lined with pure uranium.
The friends who did you dirty
May still repent. How foolish to despair!

Your sons will learn to love you when they're thirty.
This rutted road somewhere
May fork toward Tyre or Eden, who knows which?
Perhaps by next October
You will be rich,
Tactful, well-tailored, famous, slender, and sober.
Climb therefore out of that comfortable ditch
And start again upon your foot-sore travels."

Thus like a shrewd
Penelope, Hope every night unravels
His shroud of fortitude,
Coaxing him on from hurt to hurt forever;
Cries that this foaming river
On which a thousand floating relics move
Will be his last barrier before the City.
His pictures will sell, his sinuses improve,
The critics write him luminous and witty
If he but take the last, impossible stride.
There is no wholesome gust
From the world's ends can blow her from his side.
He cannot hide
To lick his wounds or seek the easy dust
But she is with him, oracles in her voice.

O! given Pandora's choice
(Or even any reasonable offer),
I would let all escape from the God's coffer
But slam the lid and lash it down with rope
Before I let go free
Malignant Hope,
The stinging mite, Man's pestilential flea.

A Garland of Precepts

Though a seeker since my birth,
Here is all I've learned on earth,
This the gist of what I know:
Give advice and buy a foe.
Random truths are all I find
Stuck like burs about my mind.
Salve a blister. Burn a letter.
Do not wash a cashmere sweater.
Tell a tale but seldom twice.
Give a stone before advice.

Pressed for rules and verities,
All I recollect are these:
Feed a cold to starve a fever.
Argue with no true believer.
Think-too-long is never-act.
Scratch a myth and find a fact.
Stitch in times saves twenty stitches.
Give the rich, to please them, riches.
Give to love your hearth and hall.
But do not give advice at all.

Epitaphs for Three Prominent Persons

THE INDEPENDENT

So open was his mind, so wide
To welcome winds from every side
That public weather took dominion,
Sweeping him bare of all opinion.

THE STATESMAN

He did not fear his enemies
  Nor their despiteful ends,
But not the seraphs on their knees
  Could save him from his friends.

THE DEMAGOGUE

That trumpet tongue which taught a nation
Loud lessons in vituperation
Teaches it yet another, viz.:
How sweet the noise of silence is.

Text for Today

A cheerful poem written upon reading in the New York Times *that Dr. Robert Cushman Murphy, of the Museum of Natural History, has discovered on Bermuda several specimens of the cahow, a bird believed extinct since 1620.*

Amid the dark that rims us now,
    Beset by news we cannot cherish,
Let us consider the cahow—
    That petrel which refused to perish,
In spite of gossip it had gone
The way of auk and mastodon.

Three hundred years ago or more,
    It built its nest, it spent its slumbers,
At ease upon Bermuda's shore
    In innocent, prolific numbers,
A creature of the coral reef
Credulous, gentle, and naïf.

But then the hungry settlers came
    To find those pastures stern for plowing.
The bird was edible and tame,
    So everybody went cahowing,
Till by and by, beside the water,
There were no more cahows to slaughter.

"Alas!" cried all the scientists,
   "Alas, career so brief and checkered!"
They crossed "cahow" from off the lists
   And wrote "extinct" upon the record.
And man could boast another feat
Of rendering nature obsolete.

But all the while, with stealth and skill
   (Necessity become its motto),
The shrewd cahow was nesting still
   On lonely rock, in cave and grotto;
Invincibly, and by some plan,
Three hundred years outwitting man.

O brave cahow, so stubborn-linked
   To your own island, palmed and surfy!
I'm happy you are not extinct,
   But got espied by Dr. Murphy.
You lend me hope, you give me joy,
Whom Total Man could not destroy.

You give me joy, you lend me hope
   (At any rate, what hope is bred on);
For surely if a bird can cope
   So cunningly with Armageddon,
And, snug in unimagined dens,
   Wait out its season for returning,
Why, so can Homo sapiens
   Tomorrow when the planet's burning—

Can flee, root, cower, scrabble, strive,
And rear its progeny. And survive.
Amid our ills that seem incurable,
Cahow, you make me feel more durable.

Journey Toward Evening

Fifty, not having expected to arrive here,
Makes a bad traveler; grows dull, complains,
Suspects the local wine, dislikes the service,
Is petulant on trains,
And thinks the climate overestimated.
Fifty is homesick, plagued by memories
Of more luxurious inns and expeditions,
Calls all lakes cold, all seas
Too tide-beset (for Fifty is no swimmer),
Nor, moving inland, likes the country more,
Believes the hills are full of snakes and brigands.
The scenery is a bore,
Like the plump, camera-hung, and garrulous trippers
Whose company henceforward he must keep.
Fifty writes letters, dines, yawns, goes up early
But not to sleep. He finds it hard to sleep.

The Angry Man

The other day I chanced to meet
An angry man upon the street—
A man of wrath, a man of war,
A man who truculently bore
Over his shoulder, like a lance,
A banner labeled "Tolerance."

And when I asked him why he strode
Thus scowling down the human road,
Scowling, he answered, "I am he
Who champions total liberty—
Intolerance being, ma'am, a state
No tolerant man can tolerate.

"When I meet rogues," he cried, "who choose
To cherish oppositional views,
Lady, like this, and in this manner,
I lay about me with my banner
Till they cry mercy, ma'am." His blows
Rained proudly on prospective foes.

Fearful, I turned and left him there
Still muttering, as he thrashed the air,
"Let the Intolerant beware!"

Midcentury Love Letter

Stay near me. Speak my name. Oh, do not wander
By a thought's span, heart's impulse, from the light
We kindle here. You are my sole defender
(As I am yours) in this precipitous night,
Which over earth, till common landmarks alter,
Is falling, without stars, and bitter cold.
We two have but our burning selves for shelter.
Huddle against me. Give me your hand to hold.

So might two climbers lost in mountain weather
On a high slope and taken by the storm,
Desperate in the darkness, cling together
Under one cloak and breathe each other warm.
Stay near me. Spirit, perishable as bone,
In no such winter can survive alone.

REFORMERS, SAINTS, AND PREACHERS

Martin Luther

Tempted by a taunting Devil,
Master Martin did his level
Best, one midnight, to combat him—
Flung a brimming inkpot at him.
Whereupon, and with a roar,
Fled the Fiend, but not before
He'd absconded, slick as whistle,
With the cautionary missile
(Having noted at a glance
All its awful puissance).

Dire the upshot! One must wince
To consider ever since
How that weapon has been hurled
Back and forth across the world
Twixt Reformer and the naughty
Devil's scribbling literati.
Ceaselessly for generations
It has spilled on men and nations
Till the mind forbears to think
Of the tides in which we sink.
Ah, the seas and seas of ink!

The Theology of Jonathan Edwards

Whenever Mr. Edwards spake
    In church about Damnation,
The very benches used to quake
    For awful agitation.

Good men would pale and roll their eyes
    While sinners rent their garments
To hear him so anatomize
    Hell's orgiastic torments,

The blood, the flames, the agonies
    In store for frail or flighty
New Englanders who did not please
    A whimsical Almighty.

Times were considered out of tune
    When half a dozen nervous
Female parishioners did not swoon
    At every Sunday service;

And, if they had been taught aright,
    Small children, carried bedwards,
Would shudder lest they meet that night
    The God of Mr. Edwards.

Abraham's God, the Wrathful One,
    Intolerant of error—
Not God the Father or the Son
    But God the Holy Terror.

The Advantages of Inaction

Philip Melanchthon
Liked, as scribe,
Logic better than diatribe.
Ascetic, lean
As Apostle Paul,
He hated a scene,
Loathed a brawl,
And looked up staunch
But temperate terms
For Luther to launch
At the Diet of Worms.

Luther laughed at him quite a lot
For his monkish ways.
"By the Lieber Gott!
Go sin a little,"
He used to roar,
"Or what can the Lord forgive you for?"
But Philip, smiling,
Paying no heed,
Went on compiling
The Augsburg Creed.

While cronies battled,
Fierce and bloody,
Philip Melanchthon kept to his study,
Praising the cool
Retreat he sat in;
Taught his school,
Polished his Latin,
Nor wielded staves
Like his fellow Germans.

Then over their graves
He preached the sermons.

The Giveaway

Saint Bridget was
A problem child.
Although a lass
Demure and mild,
And one who strove
To please her dad,
Saint Bridget drove
The family mad.
For here's the fault in Bridget lay:
She *would* give everything away.

To any soul
Whose luck was out
She'd give her bowl
Of stirabout;
She'd give her shawl,
Divide her purse
With one or all.
And what was worse,
When she ran out of things to give
She'd borrow from a relative.

Her father's gold,
Her grandsire's dinner,
She'd hand to cold
And hungry sinner;
Give wine, give meat,
No matter whose;
Take from her feet
The very shoes,
And when her shoes had gone to others,
Fetch forth her sister's and her mother's.

She could not quit.
She had to share;

Gave bit by bit
The silverware,
The barnyard geese,
The parlor rug,
Her little niece-
'S christening mug,
Even her bed to those in want,
And then the mattress of her aunt.

An easy touch
For poor and lowly,
She gave so much
And grew so holy
That when she died
Of years and fame,
The countryside
Put on her name,
And still the Isles of Erin fidget
With generous girls named Bride or Bridget.

Well, one must love her.
Nonetheless,
In thinking of her
Givingness,
There's no denial
She must have been
A sort of trial
To her kin.
The moral, too, seems rather quaint.
Who had the patience of a saint,
From evidence presented here?
Saint Bridget? Or her near and dear?

Saint Francis Borgia

OR, A REFUTATION OF HEREDITY

In Courts of Evil,
Borgias dine,
Toasting the Devil
In his own wine,
And while advances
The fiery Shade,
They ask of Francis
The renegade—
Spanish Francis,
Sport of the clan,
Born both Borgia and God-struck Man.

Doom falls shortly,
But where is he,
Francis the portly
Great Grandee?
Schooled to administer
Fief and field,
With two bars sinister
On his shield,
Life-long shaken
By Borgia pride,
He should be quaffing at Caesar's side.

Yonder, instead,
At peace he sits,
Breaking his bread
With the Jesuits,
Staking his chances
On Christian grace—
White-sheep Francis
With the Borgia face;
Of the family temper

And the family taint,
Shaping a genial Borgia saint.

When, lost and evil,
At dark of the moon,
Supping with the Devil
From a very short spoon,
Gather the Borgias, shorn of hope,
Soldier and sovereign and fat, false Pope,
They speak of Francis, and wrathful still,
They mock God's mercy
And they curse Free Will
Till wits go reeling
And thunder rolls.
But Francis, kneeling,
Prays for their souls.

Lesson for Beginners

Martin of Tours,
When he earned his shilling
Trooping the flags
Of the Roman Guard,
Came on a poor,
Aching and chilling
Beggar in rags
By the barracks yard.

Blind to his lack,
The Guard went riding.
But Martin a moment
Paused and drew
The coat from his back,
His sword from hiding,
And sabered his raiment
Into two.

Now some who muse
On the allegory
Affect to find
It a pious joke;
To beggar what use,
For Martin what glory,
In deed half-kind
And part of a cloak?

Still, it has charm
And a point worth seizing.
For all who move
In the mortal sun
Know halfway warm
Is better than freezing,
As half a love
Is better than none.

The Pastor and the Lady

Old John Knox
Of Edinburgh,
Sure of his mission
To be God's tool,
From pulpit-box
More in anger than sorrow
Called down perdition
On Female Rule.

While England wondered,
While Scotland trembled,
Hot, vociferous,
Uncontent,
John Knox thundered
To Kirk assembled

At Women's Monstriferous
Regiment.

Mary, poor creature,
Nourished in kinder
Courts and weather
Than her dour land's,
Wept that the Preacher
Had much maligned her
And wrung together
Her royal hands.

Cried Mary, "Alas,
He hails me strumpet
Whose fault is chiefly
To wear a crown!"
But his voice was the brass
Of Joshua's trumpet,
And, wavering briefly,
The walls fell down.

She lost her smile
And she lost her nation,
Lost—oh, sinister!—
Her pretty head;
Lost for a while
Her reputation,
While John Knox, Minister,
Died in bed.

Yes, leader of flocks,
Most stern and thorough,
A man well-molded
For the Scottish scene
Was old John Knox
Of Edinborough.
But would he had scolded
A plainer Queen.

Two Sides of Calvin

I. THE MARRIAGE

These are the virtues Calvin thought desirable
In a wife: an even mood,
Chastity, patience, thrift, and an untirable
Solicitude
For her lord's health. Here ends the simple list—
And not one word
Tells us if he admired a delicate wrist
Or much preferred
A hazel eye to brown or amethyst.
What! Had he not some choice
Of statures? Was he not partial in the matter
Of a right female voice,
Desire but silence or a wrenlike chatter?
And did not kindness count, or a cool repose?
A cheek of white-and-rose?
Or courtesy? Or wit?

All very well that it should not obtain
If she were fair or plain
(Since by philosophy one must admit,
In this connection,
A woman's flesh is but the spirit's mask)
But ah! not even to ask
That in her breast some taper of affection,
Some flame however decorous and dim
Should burn, and burn especially for him.

Of Mistress Calvin we know little save
She was eight years a wife,
Well-dowered, also "honorable and grave"
And lived a quiet life.
One hopes against hope that she was debonair
And managed to mingle with connubial care
For his dyspepsia, some small tendernesses.
But miracles are rare.

One's better guess is
(And all we have is Calvin's list to go on)
That since he asked, beside a sensible dot,
Only thrift, patience, chastity and so on,
Likely it's what he got.

II. A RONDEAU FOR GENEVA, 1542

In the City of God with Calvin, king,
The capital virtues had their fling,
But mirth won little or no renown.
A cold decorum, a pious frown
Were proper Burghers' appareling.

Nobody laughed much. None might sing
Or dance to fiddles or kiss-and-cling.
Condemned together were lover and clown
In the City of God.

For smiling in church, or slumbering,
For wreathing a Maypole come the Spring,
Jail was the punishment handed down.
One wonders if God, when He walked the town,
Ever felt homesick or anything
In the City of God.

How to Start a War

Said Zwingli to Muntzer,
"I'll have to be blunt, sir.
I don't like your version
Of Total Immersion.
And since God's on my side
And I'm on the dry side,
You'd better swing ovah
To me and Jehovah."

Cried Muntzer, "It's schism,
Is Infant Baptism!

Since I've had a sign, sir,
That God's will is mine, sir,
Let all men agree
With Jehovah and me,
Or go to Hell, singly,"
Said Muntzer to Zwingli,

As each drew his sword
On the side of the Lord.

Cream of the Jesters

When Philip Neri walked abroad
Beside the Tiber, praising God,
They say he was attended home
By half the younger set of Rome.

Knight, novice, scholar, boisterous boy,
They followed after him with joy,
To nurse his poor and break his bread
And hear the funny things he said.

For Philip Neri (by his birth
A Florentine) believed in mirth,
Holding that virtue took no harm
Which went with laughter arm-in-arm.

Two books he read with most affection—
The Gospels and a joke collection;
And sang hosannas set to fiddles
And fed the sick on soup and riddles.

So when the grave rebuke the merry,
Let them remember Philip Neri
(Fifteen-fifteen to ninety-five),
Who was the merriest man alive,
Then, dying at eighty or a bit,
Became a saint by Holy Wit.

Simeon Stylites

On top of a pillar Simeon sat.
He wore no mantle,
He had no hat,
But bare as a bird
Sat night and day.
And hardly a word
Did Simeon say.

Under the sun of the desert sky
He sat on a pillar
Nine feet high.
When Fool and his brother
Came round to admire,
He raised it another
Nine feet higher.

The seasons circled about his head.
He lived on water
And crusts of bread
(Or so one hears)
From pilgrims' store,
For thirty years
And a little more.

And why did Simeon sit like that,
Without a garment,
Without a hat,
In a holy rage
For the world to see?
It puzzles the age,
It puzzles me.
It puzzled many
A Desert Father.
And I think it puzzled the Good Lord, rather.

Sonnet from Assisi

Blind Francis, waiting to welcome Sister Death,
Worn though he was by ecstasies and fame,
Had heart for tune. With what remained of breath
He led his friars in canticles.

                       Then came
Brother Elias, scowling, to his side,
Small-souled Elias, crying by book and candle,
This was outrageous! Had the monks no pride?
Music at deathbeds! Ah, the shame, the scandal!

Elias gave him sermons and advice
Instead of song; which simply proves once more
What things are sure this side of paradise:
Death, taxes, and the counsel of the bore.
Though we outwit the tithe, make death our friend,
Bores we have with us even to the end.

Conversation in Avila

Teresa was God's familiar. She often spoke
To Him informally,
As if together they shared some heavenly joke.
Once, watching stormily
Her heart's ambitions wither to odds and ends,
With all to start anew,
She cried, "If this is the way You treat Your friends,
No wonder You have so few!"

There is no perfect record standing by
Of God's reply.

Origin of Species

Nicholas, Bishop of Myra's See,
Was holy a saint
As a saint could be;
Saved not a bit
Of his worldly wealth
And loved to commit
Good deeds by stealth.

Was there a poor man,
Wanting a roof?
Nicholas sheltered him weatherproof.
Who lacked a morsel
Had but to ask it
And at his doorsill
Was Nicholas' basket.

O, many a basket did he carry.
Penniless girls
Whom none would marry
Used to discover to their delight,
Into their windows
Tossed at night
(When the moon was old
And the dark was showry),
Bags of gold
Enough for a dowry.

People, I read,
Grew slightly lyrical,
Calling each deed
He did, a miracle.
Told how he calmed the sea for sailors
And rescued children
From awful jailors
Who, drawing lots
For the foul design,

Liked pickling tots
In pickle brine.

Nicholas, *circa*
Fourth cent. A.D.,
Died in the odor of sanctity.
But fortune changes,
Blessings pass,
And look what's happened to Nicholas.

He who had feared
The world's applause,
Now, with a beard,
Is Santa Claus.
A multiplied elf, he struts and poses,
Ringing up sales
In putty noses;
With Comet and Cupid
His constant partners,
Telling tall tales to kindergart'ners,
His halo fickle as
Wind and wave.

While dizzily Nicholas
Spins in his grave.

The Temptations of Saint Anthony

Off in the wilderness bare and level,
Anthony wrestled with the Devil.
Once he'd beaten the Devil down,
Anthony'd turn his eyes toward town
And leave his hermitage now and then
To come to grips with the souls of men.

Afterward, all the tales agree,
Wrestling the Devil seemed to be
Quite a relief to Anthony.

Once There Were Three Irishmen

I. COLMAN THE HERMIT

Colman of Galway,
Pledged to be
Addict of chosen poverty,
Living single in his wattled cell,
Yet had creatures
To serve him well;
Kept three friends
To cheer his house—
A cock, a fly,
And a Galway mouse.

Colman the schoolman
Told the cock:
"Crow me for Matins. Be my clock."
Said to the mouse, "At midnight creep
To wake me, praying,
From sloven sleep.
And when I read
In the Books of Grace,
Let fly hover
To keep my place."

Colman, with three
To teach or bless,
Throve in learning and holiness.
On honey and mead he fed the fly,
Praised the mouse
For his bright eye,
Bade cock follow
Where he went,
Loved the Lord
And was content.

But after a season,
One by one

As failed each small companion,
Colman, being but human still,
Wrote to the Abbot
Columcille,
"I grieve a little
On my gray rock
For fly and mouse
And the crowing cock."

Answered the Abbot
Soothingly,
"Look what a trouble wealth can be!
See how sadly is treasure bought.
While he with nothing
Mourns for naught,
You who were rich
Lament your store.
Colman, dear man,
Be rich no more."

Thenceforth, paupered
Without complaint,
Colman lived and died a saint.

II. COLUMBA THE ABBOT

Gray-eyed Columba, he
Who rhymed in the Gaelic tongue
And had been king if he cared,
Heard how over the sea
(In the place where he'd been young)
Illy the Poets fared.

"Trouble is all they make!"
Complained the angry people.
"Too heavy is their hire!
For price of a song they take
The bell from the village steeple,
The cow from the farmer's byre.

"Let them be off and going!
For mischief, for their greed,
We banish them one and all."
Then Saint Columba, knowing
A bit of the minstrel breed,
Came back to Donegal.

Back from Iona's isle
He came where the Irish heather
Was welcome to his feet.
And after a little while
He called the people together
Before the High King's seat.

"Admitted," he said, "it's so
That bards are kittle-kattle
And thorns in everyone's sides.
But who, if the Poets go,
Will sing the tale of a battle
Or the beauty of your brides?

"Like grass that autumn yellows
Your fame will wither away.
Dull must a nation be
Without these meddling fellows.
It's the price you have to pay
For owning a history."

Columba lifted his rod
And Poets walked no more
Under the exile's curse—
Colum who, next to God
And the sight of Ireland's shore,
Loved a proficient verse.

III. PATRICK THE MISSIONER

Saint Patrick was a preacher
With honey in his throat.
They say that he could charm away
A miser's dearest pence;
Could coax a feathered creature
To leave her nesting note
And fly from many a farm away
To drink his eloquence.

No Irishman was Patrick
According to the story.
The speech of Britain clung to him
(Or maybe it was Wales).
But ah, for curving rhet'ric,
Angelic oratory,
What man could match a tongue to him
Among the clashing Gaels!

Let Patrick meet a Pagan
In Antrim or Wicklow,
He'd talk to him so reachingly,
So vehement would pray,
That Cul or Neall or Reagan
Would fling aside his bow
And beg the saint beseechingly
To christen him that day.

He won the Necromancers,
The bards, the country herds.
Chief Aengus rose and went with him
To bear his staff and bowl.
For such were all his answers
To disputatious words,
Who'd parry argument with him
Would end a shriven soul.

The angry Druids muttered
A curse upon his prayers.

They sought a spell for shattering
The marvels he had done.
But Patrick merely uttered
A better spell than theirs
And sent the Druids scattering
Like mist before the sun.

They vanished like the haze on
The plume of the fountain.
But still their scaly votaries
Were venomous at hand.
So three nights and days on
Tara's stony mountain
He thundered till those coteries
Of serpents fled the land.

Grown old but little meeker
At length he took his rest.
And centuries have listened, dumb,
To tales of his renown.
For Ireland loves a speaker,
So loves Saint Patrick best:
The only man in Christendom
Has talked the Irish down.

The Thunderer

God's angry man, His crotchety scholar,
Was Saint Jerome,
The great name-caller,
Who cared not a dime
For the laws of libel
And in his spare time
Translated the Bible.
Quick to disparage
All joys but learning,
Jerome thought marriage
Better than burning;

But didn't like woman's
Painted cheeks;
Didn't like Romans,
Didn't like Greeks,
Hated Pagans
For their Pagan ways,
Yet doted on Cicero all his days.

A born reformer, cross and gifted,
He scolded mankind
Sterner than Swift did;
Worked to save
The world from the heathen;
Fled to a cave
For peace to breathe in,
Promptly *where*with
For miles around
He filled the air with
Fury and sound.
In a mighty prose
For almighty ends,
He thrust at his foes,
Quarreled with his friends,
And served his Master,
Though with complaint.
He wasn't a plaster
Sort of saint.

But he swelled men's minds
With a Christian leaven.
It takes all kinds
To make a Heaven.

Paterfamilias

Of all the saints who have won their charter—
Holy man, hero, hermit, martyr,
Mystic, missioner, sage, or wit—
Saint Thomas More is my favorite.
For he loved these bounties with might and main:
God and his house and his little wife, Jane,
And four fair children his heart throve on,
Margaret, Elizabeth, Cecily, and John.

That More was a good man everybody knows.
He sang good verses and he wrote good prose,
Enjoyed a good caper and liked a good meal
And made a good Master of the Privy Seal.
A friend to Erasmus, Lily's friend,
He lived a good life and he had a good end
And left good counsel for them to con,
Margaret, Elizabeth, Cecily, and John.

Some saints are alien, hard to love,
Wild as an eagle, strange as a dove,
Too near to heaven for the mind to scan.
But Thomas More was a family man,
A husband, a courtier, a doer and a hoper
(Admired of his son-in-law, Mr. Roper),
Who punned in Latin like a Cambridge don
With Margaret, Elizabeth, Cecily, and John.

It was less old Henry than Anne Boleyn
Hailed him to the Tower and locked him in.
But even in the Tower he saw things brightly.
He spoke to his jailers most politely,
And while the sorrowers turned their backs
He rallied the headsman who held the ax,
Then blessed, with the blessing of Thomas More,
God and his garden and his children four.

And I fear they missed him when he was gone—
Margaret, Elizabeth, Cecily, and John.

For a Boy Named Sebastian

Stamped as you are both His and Hers,
    My child, you do not greatly need
Godmothers or Astrologers
    Or gentlemen of Merlin's breed
Around your crib to prophecy
What way your fortunes lie.

The stars have danced, the eagles spread
    Benign and intellectual wings
For augury. Upon your head
    Must fall a rain of pleasant things.
Still, while good wishes stream on you,
Accept mine, too.

For I recall your name-saint. He
    Won some renown, however narrow,
By getting pierced incessantly
    With Everyman's ungracious arrow.
He owned no armor but his skin
And that, too thin.

Now none can fend all barbs away
    Even with candle, book and bell.
But this my hope, Sebastian: May
    You grow a noble sort of shell,
A good, tough, weapon-blunting hide
To stow your heart inside,

Not made of coarseness or conceit,
    Not dull or cold or overbearing,
But proudly masculine and neat—
    One suitable for princely wearing.
Then, though you feel the arrows' touch,
They can not harm you much,
Or turn you off from any issue.

And that's the best wish I can wish you.

A CERTAIN AGE

Girl's-Eye View of Relatives

FIRST LESSON

The thing to remember about fathers is, they're men.
A girl has to keep it in mind.
They are dragon-seekers, bent on improbable rescues.
Scratch any father, you find
Someone chock-full of qualms and romantic terrors,
Believing change is a threat—
Like your first shoes with heels on, like your first bicycle
It took such months to get.

Walk in strange woods, they warn you about the snakes there.
Climb, and they fear you'll fall.
Books, angular boys, or swimming in deep water—
Fathers mistrust them all.
Men are the worriers. It is difficult for them
To learn what they must learn:
How you have a journey to take and very likely,
For a while, will not return.

42

TURN OF THE SCREW

Girl cousins condescend. They wear
Earrings, and dress like fashion's sample,
Have speaking eyes and curly hair.
And parents point to their example.
But the boy cousins one's allotted
Are years too young for one. Or spotted.

TRIOLET AGAINST SISTERS

Sisters are always drying their hair.
   Locked into rooms, alone,
They pose at the mirror, shoulders bare,
Trying this way and that their hair,
Or fly importunate down the stair
   To answer a telephone.
Sisters are always drying their hair,
   Locked into rooms, alone.

IN PRAISE OF AUNTS

Of all that tribe the young must do
Familial obedience to,
Whom we salute on anniversaries,
Whose names we learn while new in nurseries
Or borrow at baptismal fonts,
The soothingest are aunts.

Aunts are discreet, a little shy
By instinct. They forbear to pry
Into recesses of the spirit
Where apprehensions lie.
Yet, given a tale to hear, they *hear* it.

Aunts spinster pamper us with praise,
And seats for worldly matinées
With coffee after. Married aunts,
Attentive to material wants,

Run rather to the shared comestible,
Taboo or indigestible;
Are lenient but cool;
And let us, if we must, play fool.

Aunts carry no duty in their faces.
Their letters, mailed from far-off places,
Are merely letters meant to read
(Answerable at a moderate speed),
Not cries of need
Or vessels heavy with their hopes.
Aunts also send,
Tucked into casual envelopes,
Money entirely ours to spend.

At night they do not lie awake
Shuddering for our sorrows' sake.
Beneath our flesh we seldom wear
Their skeletons, nor need we stare
Into a looking glass and see
Their images begin to be.
Aunts care, but only mildly care,
About our winter moods,
Postures, or social attitudes,
And whether we've made a friend or dropped one.

All should have aunts, or else adopt one.

THE ADVERSARY

A mother's hardest to forgive.
Life is the fruit she longs to hand you,
Ripe on a plate. And while you live,
Relentlessly she understands you.

A Certain Age

All of a sudden, bicycles are toys,
Not locomotion. Bicycles are for boys
And seventh-graders, screaming when they talk.
A girl would rather
Take vows, go hungry, put on last year's frock,
Or dance with her own father
Than pedal down the block.

This side of childhood lies a narrow land,
Its laws unwritten, altering out of hand,
But, more than Sparta's, savagely severe.
Common or gentry,
The same taboos prevail. One learns, by ear,
The customs of the country
Or pays her forfeit here.

No bicycles. No outcast dungarees
Over this season's round and scarless knees,
No soft departures from the veering norm.
But the same bangle,
Marked with a nickname, now from every arm
Identically must dangle,
The speech be uniform—

Uniform as the baubles round the throat,
The ill-made wish, the stiffened petticoat,
And beauty, blurred but burning in the face.
Now, scrubbed and scented,
They move together toward some meeting place,
Wearing a regimented,
Unutterable grace.

They travel rapt, each compass pointing south—
Heels to the shoes and lipstick on the mouth.

Bootless Speculations

One fact eccentric I often muse on:
Girls of sixteen won't keep their shoes on.

Girls, at sixteen, for all our strictures,
Are proper as Puritans,
Pretty as pictures.
With waists cinched tightly,
Wearing ponytails,
They move more lightly
Than a ship with sails,
Than roses shaking
The summer dews off—
But why must they always be taking their shoes off?

Girls of sixteen
Have rows and rows
Of fanciful, lean
Capezios.
Helter-skelter,
To point of scandal,
Their closets shelter
Slipper and sandal,
Glass shoes, gilt shoes,
Shoes with baubles on,
Three-inch-stilt shoes
That anyone wobbles on,
Shoes gone risible,
Shoes for sport,
Shoes without visible
Means of support.
Each maidenly foot is a clad-with-care foot,
But how do they go?
Why, chiefly barefoot.

They never enter
Their entrance halls

But front and center
The footwear falls:
Pumps under sofas;
Brogues on the stairs;
Loathsome loafers
Beneath wing chairs;
Shoes on the landing,
Lost in flight;
On porches standing
Overnight,
While, legs a-taper,
Combing their curls,
Blithely caper
The discalced girls.
Shoeless they chatter their gossip windy
Or barefoot at parties
Dance the Lindy.

Girls at sixteen have depths unsounded.
Of sugar and spice
Are they compounded;
Sweetly their powers
Shame doubting Thomases;
They keep late hours
But keep their promises;
They keep cool heads
For the course they cruise on.
So why in the world can't they keep their shoes on?

Portrait of Girl with Comic Book

Thirteen's no age at all. Thirteen is nothing.
It is not wit, or powder on the face,
Or Wednesday matinées, or misses' clothing,
Or intellect, or grace.
Twelve has its tribal customs. But thirteen
Is neither boys in battered cars nor dolls,
Not *Sara Crewe,* or movie magazine,
Or pennants on the walls.

Thirteen keeps diaries and tropical fish
(A month, at most); scorns jumpropes in the spring;
Could not, would fortune grant it, name its wish;
Wants nothing, everything;
Has secrets from itself, friends it despises;
Admits none to the terrors that it feels;
Owns half a hundred masks but no disguises;
And walks upon its heels.

Thirteen's anomalous—not that, not this:
Not folded bud, or wave that laps a shore,
Or moth proverbial from the chrysalis.
Is the one age defeats the metaphor.
Is not a town, like childhood, strongly walled
But easily surrounded; is no city.
Nor, quitted once, can it be quite recalled—
Not even with pity.

Launcelot with Bicycle

Her window looks upon the lane.
From it, anonymous and shy,
Twice daily she can see him plain,
Wheeling heroic by.
She droops her cheek against the pane
And gives a little sigh.

Above him maples at their bloom
Shake April pollen down like stars
While he goes whistling past her room
Toward unimagined wars,
A tennis visor for his plume,
Scornful of handlebars.

And, counting over in her mind
His favors, gleaned like windfall fruit
(A morning when he spoke her kind,
An afterschool salute,
A number that she helped him find,
Once, for his paper route),

Sadly she twists a stubby braid
And closer to the casement leans—
A wistful and a lily maid
In moccasins and jeans,
Despairing from the seventh grade
To match his lordly teens.

And so she grieves in Astolat
(Where other girls have grieved the same)
For being young and therefore not
Sufficient to his fame—
Who will by summer have forgot
Grief, April, and his name.

Homework for Annabelle

$A = bh$ over 2.
   3.14 is π.
But I'd forgotten, if I ever knew,
   What $R's$ divided by.
Though I knew once, I'd forgotten clean
What a girl must study to reach fifteen—
How V is Volume and M's for Mass,
And the hearts of the young are brittle as glass.

I had forgotten, and half with pride,
   Fifteen's no field of clover.
So there I sit at Annabelle's side,
   Learning my lessons over.
For help is something you have to give
When daughters are faced with the Ablative
Or first encounter in any school
Immutable gender's mortal rule.

Day after day for a weary spell,
   When the dusk has pitched its tents,
I sit with a book and Annabelle
   At the hour of confidence
And rummage for lore I had long consigned
To cobwebby attics of my mind,
Like: For the Radius, write down R,
The Volga's a river, Vega's a star,
Brazil's in the Tropic of Capricorn,
And heart is a burden that has to be borne.

Oh, high is the price of parenthood,
   And daughters may cost you double.
You dare not forget, as you thought you could,
   That youth is a plague and trouble.
N times 7 is $7n$—
Here I go learning it all again:

The climates of continents tend to vary,
The verb "to love" 's not auxiliary,
Tomorrow will come and today will pass,
But the hearts of the young are brittle as glass.

Fourteenth Birthday

The Enemy, who wears
Her mother's usual face
And confidential tone,
Has access; doubtless stares
Into her writing case
And listens on the phone.

Her fortress crumbles. Spies
Who call themselves her betters
Harry her night and day.
Herself's the single prize.
Likely they read her letters
And bear the tale away,

Or eavesdrop on her sleep
(Uncountered and unchidden)
To learn her dreams by heart.
There is no lock will keep
A secret rightly hidden
From their subversive art.

But till the end is sure,
Till on some open plain
They bring her to her knees,
She'll face them down—endure
In silence and disdain
Love's utmost treacheries.

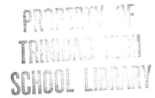

PROPERTY OF
TRINIDAD HIGH
SCHOOL LIBRARY

11, 08 2

Ballade of Lost Objects

Where are the ribbons I tie my hair with?
    Where is my lipstick? Where are my hose—
The sheer ones hoarded these weeks to wear with
    Frocks the closets do not disclose?
Perfumes, petticoats, sports chapeaux,
    The blouse Parisian, the earring Spanish—
Everything suddenly ups and goes.
    And where in the world did the children vanish?

This is the house I used to share with
    Girls in pinafores, shier than does.
I can recall how they climbed my stair with
    Gales of giggles, on their toptoes.
Last seen wearing both braids and bows
    (But looking rather Raggedy-Annish),
When they departed nobody knows—
    Where in the world did the children vanish?

Two tall strangers, now I must bear with,
    Decked in my personal furbelows,
Raiding the larder, rending the air with
    Gossip and terrible radios.
Neither my friends nor quite my foes,
    Alien, beautiful, stern, and clannish,
Here they dwell, while the wonder grows:
    Where in the world did the children vanish?

Prince, I warn you, under the rose,
    Time is the thief you cannot banish.
These are my daughters, I suppose.
    But where in the world did the children vanish?

The Doll House

After the children left it, after it stood
For a while in the attic,
Along with the badminton set, and the skis too good
To be given away, and the Peerless Automatic
Popcorn Machine that used to fly into rages,
And the Dr. Dolittle books, and the hamsters' cages,
She brought it down once more
To a bedroom, empty now, on the second floor
And put the furniture in.
                    There was nothing much
That couldn't be used again with a bit of repair.
It was all there,
Perfect and little and inviolate.
So, with the delicate touch
A jeweler learns, she mended the rocking chair,
Meticulously laundered
The gossamer parlor curtains, dusted the grate,
Glued the glazed turkey to the flowered plate,
And polished the Lilliput writing desk.
                    She squandered
One bold October day and half the night
Binding the carpets round with a ribbon border;
Till, to her grave delight
(With the kettle upon the stove, the mirror's face
Scoured, the formal sofa set in its place),
She saw the dwelling decorous and in order.

It was a good house. It had been artfully built
By an idle carpenter once, when the times were duller.
The windows opened and closed. The knocker was gilt.
And every room was painted a suitable color
Or papered to scale
For the sake of the miniature Adam and Chippendale.
And there were proper hallways,
Closets, lights, and a staircase. (What had always

Pleased her most
Was the tiny, exact, mahogany newel post.)
And always, too, wryly she thought to herself,
Absently pinning
A drapery's pleat, smoothing a cupboard shelf—
Always, from the beginning,
This outcome had been clear. Ah! She had known
Since the first clapboard was fitted, first rafter hung
(Yet not till now had known that she had known),
This was no daughters' fortune but her own—
Something cautiously lent to the careless young
To dazzle their cronies with for a handful of years
Till the season came
When their toys diminished to programs and souvenirs,
To tousled orchids, diaries well in arrears,
Anonymous snapshots stuck round a mirror frame,
Or letters locked away.
                          Now seed of the past
Had fearfully flowered. Wholly her gift at last,
Here was her private estate, a peculiar treasure
Cut to her fancy's measure.
Now there was none to trespass, no one to mock
The extravagance of her sewing or her spending
(The tablecloth stitched out of lace, the grandfather's clock,
Stately upon the landing,
With its hands eternally pointing to ten past five).

Now all would thrive.

Over this house, most tranquil and complete,
Where no storm ever beat,
Whose innocent stair
No messenger ever climbed on quickened feet
With tidings either of rapture or of despair,
She was sole mistress. Through the panes she was able
To peer at her world reduced to the size of dream
But pure and unaltering.
                          There stood the dinner table,
Invincibly agleam

With the undisheveled candles, the flowers that bloomed
Forever and forever,
The wine that never
Spilled on the cloth or sickened or was consumed.

The *Times* lay at the doorsill, but it told
Daily the same unstirring report. The fire
Painted upon the hearth would not turn cold,
Or the constant hour change, or the heart tire
Of what it must pursue,
Or the guest depart, or anything here be old.

"Nor ever," she whispered, "bid the spring adieu."

And caught into this web of quietnesses
Where there was neither After nor Before,
She reached her hand to stroke the unwithering grasses
Beside the small and incorruptible door.

Lament for Lost Lodgings

"Do you remember an Inn, Miranda?" —*Hilaire Belloc, "Tarantella."*

Yes, do you remember an Inn,
Miranda,
Where chairs rocked, creaking,
On the long veranda,
Where beds were elderly
To match the plumbing
But the manager smiled at our coming?

Far from the highway where the traffic muttered,
It was clapboarded white,
It was greenly shuttered.
There peace descended
When night began
And we paid by American Plan.

Remember the lobster redder than the wine,
The breakfast dining-room
That closed at nine,
The wavy mirrors
In the first-floor Women's,
The waistresses all from Smith or Simmons
And the crickets loud
But the busboys louder

And the reek of the leek
In the weekly chowder
And the carefree luggage
That porters brought in
And the baths you could launch a yacht in?

Nevermore, Miranda, nevermore.
Only the faceless,
Duplicated door
Of a thousand Motels
From Taos to Truro
With Television built in the built-in bureau.
Only the wallpaper, self-assertive,
And the dusty coming
And the going, furtive,
And the Howard Johnson's
For a meal, en masse,
And the clink of the drink
In the toothbrush glass.
Only the guests, neither gentlemen nor ladies,
But Messieur the Buick
Or Madame, Mercedes
And the fee in advance
And the sleeping pill
For the traffic roaring at the sill.

Let me fly to an Inn like a sword to its scabbard
Where the crickets cry
And the walls are clapboard.
Till I find a rocker
On a long veranda
I'll motor no more, Miranda.

New England Pilgrimage

THE CUSTOMS OF THE COUNTRY

Connecticut, with much at stake,
Prefers to call a pool a lake,
But in New Hampshire and beyond
They like to call a lake a pond.

LANDSCAPE WITH FIGURINES

Vermont has mountains,
Vermont has pines,
Has highways innocent of billboard signs,
Has white front porches, neighborly and wandering,
Where ladies hang the laundry
When they feel like laundering.

People in Vermont
Keep their tongues well-throttled,
Have carbonated summertimes that should be bottled,
Have cows like goddesses and cats like pandas.
But they *will* hang their washing
On their front verandas.

HAPPY TIME

It goes to the heart,
It goes to the head
To look on lobster
When it's red.
Lobster, native on a *carte du jour,* may
Make a gourmand out of a gourmet.

THEATER-IN-THE-BARN

Old Guernsey ghosts—do they recall, with shock,
When they were the sole stars of summer stock?

MEMO FOR DUNCAN HINES

Russians are fond of caviar.
  The French, whom nothing ruffles,
Admire the pale
Reclusive snail,
  And send their pigs for truffles.
The Swedes hold court
With smorgasbord.
  But down New England way,
Where once the bean
Was high cuisine,
  Behold the Relish Tray!

>   *Don't look now,*
>   *But here it comes:*
>   *Cinnamon apples,*
>   *Candied plums,*
>   *Fanciful notions*
>   *Like pickled peas,*
>   *And oceans and oceans*
>   *Of cottage cheese.*

I've ordered oysters on the Cape
  When empty was the bucket.
The chowder bowl
That soothes the soul
  Has failed me in Nantucket.
I've found Vermont
At times in want
  Of turkey, which was hellish.
But who has been
At any Inn
  Immaculate of Relish?

>   *Dine at Danbury,*
>   *Lunch at Noone.*
>   *A similar cranberry*
>   *Stains the spoon.*

It's onions at Dover
To spice the breeze,
And over and over
It's cottage cheese.

There's many a gastronomic gulf
  No alien palate bridges.
On Britain's coast
They toast their toast,
  Then cool it in their fridges.
Chinese say grace
Above a brace
  Of birds' nest rolled in batter.
But, Haddam Neck
To the Kennebec,
  There reigns the Relish Platter.

Butter your muffin,
Order your filet,
Harbor your strength
For the piccalilli,
For things in an umber
Mustard mix,
The sweet cucumber,
The carrot sticks,
The celery twisted
Like tropic trees,
And the cottage cheese.
And the cottage cheese.

AFTERNOON TEA AT THE COLONY

In Peterboro or on its margin
  (Where I was visiting at),
I watched the authors roaming at large in
  Their natural habitat.
Tranced, on the slopes of the Great McDow'll,
I saw them feed, I heard them growl.
But try as I would, I couldn't tell
Which was lion
And which gazelle.

SIC TRANSIT

Although these days it makes my hair lift—
Descending Mansfield in a chair lift—
Now (over twenty-one and freeborn)
I'd rather ride down than be ski-borne.

CONCERNING MAINE SWIMMING

Glacial and glittery,
The waters off Kittery.
I dread to dunk
At Kennebunk.
But that cool wave
Past Bath and Bristol
I wouldn't brave
At the point of a pistol.

A Dream of Gifties

Somewhere somebody sits
   (In a cave, in a cell, in a tower) —
Somebody out of his wits
   But primed with lunatic power.
And what is he doing when midnight's brewing
   And mocking moons sail high?
Inventing with sneers the Souvenirs
   That summer tourists buy;
With sneers and jeers and lunatic leers
Inventing the roadside Souvenirs
   That motoring tourists buy:

Balsam pillows in dubious felts,
Handpainted neckties,
Wampum belts,
Perfumes harsher
Than laws by Dracon,
Plates with pictures of Echo Lake on,
Pottery gnomes for cluttering yards
And plaid, unplayable playing-cards.

No Gift Shop stands so bleak,
   Motel so poor but has'm,
From Pike's memorial peak
   To dark Ausable Chasm.
At soda fountains in the Rocky Mountains,
   At southern inns gardenious,
Behold rich rows of the curios
   Spawned by his nightmare genius:

Pots of cactuses, gray and scratchy,
Moccasins spurned
By the poorest Apache,
Incense burners
Like skulls and hearses,
Raffia baskets, raffia purses,

Leather-work calendars slightly singed,
And all designed by a mind unhinged.

They lurk with a smirk obscene
    In a thousand Parks and Grottos
Where all of the soap is green
    And all of the mugs wear mottos.
From seashore tavern to Carlsbad Cavern,
    Wherever the Buicks roam,
You can trace his tracks by the pennants and plaques
    That motorists carry home,
The terrible stacks of pennants and plaques
That ladies in slacks with sunburnt backs
    Bemusedly carry home,

While he laughs Ha Ha and he snorts Hey Hey.
Oh, I had a horrible
Thought today!
When soon our astronauts
Raid the stars,
What will they fetch from the fields of Mars?
Souvenir spoons in a matching set
And a pink Saint Christopher statuette.

A Tour of English Cathedrals

IN THE SUMMER (OR RAINY) SEASON

WESTMINSTER ABBEY

I wandered lonely as a fareless cabby
Through miles and miles of the Royal Abbey,
Which some call stately and some call sinister
But most Americans call "Westminister,"
For I wanted to see, beneath the throne,
That Stone of Scone which is Scotland's Stone.

The Stone was the reason for my safari,
But, getting confused by the statuary,
By the granite poets and the marble dukes,
By generals and judges in carved perukes,
By king in his coffin, by knight in his stall,
I didn't see the Stone of Scone at all.

Though later, in a buttery, pondering alone,
I was served by the waitress with a scone of stone.

ST. PAUL'S

From the stone gallery there's a view
    Of London that is simply heaven.
To see it, all you have to do
    Is climb six hundred twenty-seven
Steps. It doesn't cost a penny.
The only thing is I found it exactly six hundred and
    twenty-six steps too many.

ELY

Although assembled of various famous styles,
And one of the vastest in all of the British Isles,
Ely, whenever it rains,
Makes one aware of the drains—
For the Master Builders, while certainly up and coming,
Didn't understand plumbing.

WELLS

All by themselves on the Bishop's Moat,
Two swans were somnolently afloat
Who didn't seem to care in particular
If naves were Gothic or Perpendicular,
Or faced with limestone or Purbeck marble,
But only that weather had stopped being horr'ble
And sun, for a moment, was edging through.
Then, prying a pebble out of my shoe,
I trudged off churchward to stare for a while
At the Tombs of the Saxons on the Northern Aisle.

NOTE ON THE PREVALENCE OF FEE-TAKING

I think in all of England's See
No verger dwells untipped by me.

SALISBURY

Salisbury had a splendid steeple,
    A cloister walk in good repair,
And lots of French and German people
    Reading their guidebooks everywhere.
Despite a rather ominous sky,
They all took pictures. So did I.

We loved the Chapter House; its gate
    Looked toward a river and a thicket.
Now, *was* it Salisbury where we ate
    A sole that wasn't quite the ticket,
Or farther on, at Bath? No matter—
It's where I found my Lowestoft platter.

NOTE ON THE PREVALENCE OF CHORISTERS

Nothing can glower
    Like a tourist throng
Trapped for an hour
    By Evensong.

SOME NOTES ON THE PREVALENCE OF
SEVENTEENTH-CENTURY CHURCHES

A couple of very industrious men
Were Grinling Gibbons and Christopher Wren.
Across the land,
While the nation gulped,
Christopher planned
And Grinling sculped,
Busy as bees in honeycombs.
Colonnades, porticoes, elegant domes,
Apses, transepts, naves, and chapels,
Pulpits and choirs with turned pineapples,
Pews of mahogany, ceilings of gilt—
Grinling carved as Christopher built,
All over England, an absolute host of them.
And I think by now I must have seen most of them.

CANTERBURY TALE

When April's dulcet showers begin,
Few rooms are free at the Falstaff Inn.
In May, in June, when bloom the roses,
The Abbot's Barton's guest list closes.
Comes on July, you'll find small bounty
Remaining at the cozy County.
But when sets in the August flurry,
Fly, Pilgrim, fly from Canterbury!

WINCHESTER

When we came into Winchester,
    Unsuppered and morose,
We saw a hundred swallows
    Fly circling in the Close.

Down the austere gray corridors
    No footsteps rang but ours,
And all the airs of evening
    Were spiced with gillyflowers.

Against the Canon's Garden
    A red-and-white marquee
Stood, gala, for tomorrow's
    Old Boys' and Parents' Tea,

And it had rained that morning,
    Would rain again that night,
But nothing then save silence
    Spoke in the colored light

Till a bird sang his Vespers
    From somewhere near at hand.
Then, suddenly, in focus
    We saw this Fortress stand,

This plot, this realm, this England,
    And truly wished it well
Before we sought in Winchester
    Our bleak two-star hotel.

A Word to Hostesses

Celebrities are lonely when
They congregate with lesser men.
Among less lambent men they sit,
Bereft of style, deprived of wit,
A little chilly to the touch,
And do not sparkle very much.

Wrenched from their coteries, they lack
Mirrors to send their image back,
And find it, therefore, hard to muster
Glint for a purely private luster.
(One sees a hunger in their eyes
For splendor they can recognize.)

But seat them next a Name, and lo!
How they most instantly will glow,
Will light the sky or heat the room
With gossip's incandescent bloom,
As if, like twigs, they only burst
In flame when rubbed together first.

Hostesses, then, when you are able
To lure Celebrity to table,
It is discreet to bear in mind
He needs the comfort of his kind.

Fetch other Names. Fetch three or four.
A dozen's better, or a score.
And half a hundred might be fitter.

But even one will make him glitter.

Spectator's Guide to Contemporary Art

HOW TO TELL PORTRAITS FROM STILL-LIFES

Ladies whose necks are long and swanny
Are always signed Modigliani.
But flowers explosive in a crock?
Braque.

ON THE FARTHER WALL, MARC CHAGALL

One eye without a head to wear it
Sits on the pathway, and a chicken,
Pursued perhaps by astral ferret,
Flees, while the plot begins to thicken.
Two lovers kiss. Their hair is kelp.
Nor are the titles any help.

THE GOLDEN TOUCH

Señor Dali,
  Born delirious,
Considers it folly
  To be serious;
Would rather paint than cubes or cones
Mona Williams and telephones—
Not toothsome fruits or tender trilliums
But melting watches and Mrs. Williams,
With an extra flourish to "Dali—*his* mark"
Now that she's Mona, Countess Bismarck.

THE MODERN PALETTE

Picasso's Periodic hue
   Is plain enough for any dullard.
The simple red succeeds the blue,
   And now the Party-colored.

SQUEEZE PLAY

Jackson Pollock had a quaint
Way of saying to his sibyl,
"Shall I dribble?
Should I paint?"
And with never an instant's quibble,
Sibyl always answered,
"Dribble."

THE CASUAL LOOK

In pictures by Grandma Moses
The people have no noses.

Publisher's Party

At tea in cocktail weather,
   The lady authors gather.
Their hats are made of feather.
   They talk of Willa Cather.

They talk of Proust and Cather,
   And how we drift, and whither.
Where wends the lady author,
   Martinis do not wither.

Their cocktails do not wither
   Nor does a silence hover.
That critic who comes hither
   Is periled like a lover;

Is set on like a lover.
 Alert and full of power,
They flush him from his cover,
 No matter where he cower.

And Honor Guest must cower
 When they, descending rather
Like bees upon a flower,
 Demand his views on Cather—

On Wharton, James, or Cather,
 Or Eliot or Luther,
Or Joyce or Cotton Mather,
 Or even Walter Reuther.

In fact, the tracts of Reuther
 They will dispute together
For hours, gladly, soother
 Than fall on silent weather.

From teas in any weather
Where lady authors gather,
Whose hats are largely feather,
Whose cocktails do not wither,
Who quote from Proust and Cather
(With penitence toward neither),
Away in haste I slither,
Feeling I need a breather.

Notes on Some Eminent Foreign Novelists

FROM ANY ANGLE IT'S A VIPER'S TANGLE

The wise commit the errors,
The good commit the sins.
The brave are full of terrors.
Only the loser wins.
And even white is partly black
In books by François Mauriac.

THE MUTED SCREEN OF GRAHAM GREENE

Were all our sins so empty of enjoyment,
All sinners gloomy as the ones he paints,
The Devil soon, I think, would lack employment
And the earth teem with saints.

THE CAT ON THE MAT DESERVES A PAT

Colette
Kept Love for a pet,
Brushed its fur as soft as silk,
Gave it saucerfuls of milk,
Taught it all the tricks there are—
But didn't trust it very far.

LAST YEAR'S DISCUSSION: THE NOBEL RUSSIAN

In Fond du Lac, Bronxville, Butte, Chicago,
Everyone ordered Dr. Zhivago,
A novel by Boris Pasternak.

But how many read it from front to back
In Bronxville, Chicago, Butte, Fond du Lac?

THE ABSOLUTE LAW OF EVELYN WAUGH

Englishmen of the upper classes
Are more amusing than the masses.

Mrs. Sweeney Among the Allegories

*Multi-level verses composed in a New Haven Railroad car immedi-
ately after having spent an afternoon with the* Collected Poems *of*
T. S. Eliot *and an evening at* The Confidential Clerk.

I

In the beginning was the word
   And, for an act, I understood.
Colby was Lord Mulhammer's son.
   Burnished Lucasta longed for food.

Gnomic, the jests of Ina Claire
   Scampered on super-cadenced feet.
Eggerson spoke of Brussels Sprouts.
   Entered, at left, the Paraclete.

Defunctive message under B.
   Passed comprehension after while,
Nearly; even I could see
   Discussion animate the aisle.

Transfigured, the illicit clerk
   Refused a post designed for him.
Play beneath play beneath a play
   Then burnt, just visible but dim.

II

"This music crept by me upon the water,"
Along Times Square, cutting through Shubert Alley.
O! Poet's Poet, for a bit I heard,
Upon a little stool in the Algonquin,
The murmur of your transcendental meaning,
With all the fiddles of the mind beginning
To scratch it out. But then,
A single waiter with insomnia cried,
"Madam, your double bourbon," and it died.

III

On the stage the actors come and go.
Whose heir is which they do not know.

IV

Between the Idea
And the Interpretation,
Between the epigram
And the guffaw,
            Falls the Symbol.

Between the Intermission
And the Finale,
Between the horns
And the dilemma,
            Falls the Symbol.

Between the First Level
And the Third Level,
Between the dark
And the daylight,
Between Grand Central Terminal
And Larchmont, New York,
            Falls the Symbol.

        Here, then, is the story:

V

T. Eliot, the Anglican, who feared God,
    Removing his bowler, furling his umbrella,
Set down, in riddles, dogma for the crowd.
    Now he's in Africa with another fella,
Leaving behind no confidential Glossary.
I hope he's not run over by Rhinosauri.

VI

For
This is the way his farce ends,
This is the way his farce ends,
This is the way his farce ends,
Not with a mot but a moral.

Lines Scribbled on a Program

AND DISCOVERED BY A WAITER SWEEPING UP
AFTER A LITERARY DINNER

Whenever public speakers rise
 To dazzle hearers and beholders,
A film comes over both my eyes.
 Inevitably, toward my shoulders
I feel my head begin to sink.
It is an allergy, I think.

No matter what the time or place,
 No matter how adroit the speaker
Or rich the tone or famed the face,
 I feel my life force ebbing weaker.
Even the chairman, lauding him,
Can make the room about me swim.

The room swims. And my palms are wet.
 Languor and lassitude undo me.
I fumble with a cigarette
 For ashtrays never handy to me,
Lift chin, grit teeth, shift in my chair,
But nothing helps—not even prayer.

From all who Talk, I dream away—
 From statesmen heavy with their travels,
From presidents of P.T.A.
 Exchanging honorary gavels;
From prelate, pedant, wit, and clown,
Club treasurer, John Mason Brown;

From lecturers on the ductless gland,
 Ex-Communists, ex-dukes, exhorters,
Poets with poems done by hand,
 Political ladies, lady reporters,
Professors armed with bell and book,
Mimes, magnates, mayors, Alistair Cooke.

The hot, the fluent, and the wise,
   The dull, the quick-upon-the-trigger—
Alike, alike they close my eyes.
   Alike they rob me of my vigor.
For me Demosthenes, with pain,
Had mouthed his Attic stones in vain.

The aforementioned being clear
   Concerning speech, concerning speaker,
Alas, what am I doing here,
   Facing my empty plate and beaker,
And watching with a wild unrest
The rising of the evening's Guest?
Ah, was it mine, this monstrous choice?
Whose accents these? And whose the voice
That wakes in me a pang well known?

Good God, it is my own, my own!

Speaking of Television

THE LAST WORD

I'd take more pleasure in discussions schola'ly
If Bergen Evans wouldn't laugh so jollily.

PICKWICK TIME

Readings by Mr. Laughton
I cannot dote as I ought on.
Though the prose is doubtless
Deathless,
Could he not speak out less
Breathless?

ALMOST ANY EVENING

On all the channels,
Nothing but panels!

INSULT IS THE SOUL OF WIT

Groucho Marx is a man I'm fond of.
A gray-haired jest he can make a blonde of.
But I'd rather be a derelict, sleeping in parks,
Than a guest on the program of Groucho Marx.

DEFINITION OF AN AFTERNOON PROGRAM

A lady who shows you how to embellish
Saturday's roast with Monday's relish.

ON THE PREVALENCE OF MURDER

Did I hear you say
Crime doesn't *pay?*

BY ANY OTHER NAME

A pretty pair
I like to praise
Are Peter Lind
And Mary Hayes.
Excuse it, please—
What I meant, really,
Was Linda Hayes
And Peter Healy.
No, no!
I'm coming all unpinned.
It's Healy Hayes
And Mary Lind,
Or anyhow
Some close relation.
Ah, well! Let's try another station.

ROBIN HOOD

Zounds, gramercy, and rootity-toot!
Here comes the man in the green flannel suit.

THE $64,000 ANSWER

I think that I shall never see
A Quiz Tot who appeals to me.

REFLECTIONS DENTAL

How pure, how beautiful, how fine
Do teeth on television shine!
No flutist flutes, no dancer twirls,
But comes equipped with matching pearls.
Gleeful announcers all are born
With sets like rows of hybrid corn.
Clowns, critics, clergy, commentators,
Ventriloquists and roller skaters,
M.C.s who beat their palms together,
The girl who diagrams the weather,
The crooner crooning for his supper—
All flash white treasures, lower and upper.
With miles of smiles the airwaves teem,
And each an orthodontist's dream.

'Twould please my eye as gold a miser's—
One charmer with uncapped incisors.

THE IMPORTANCE OF BEING WESTERN

Wyatt Earp
Rides tall in the stearp.

THE PERRY COMO SHOW

Someday, perhaps,
Will he really collapse?

MAMA

The humor of family sagas is far from Shavian—
Including the Scandinavian.

THE NEWS

Now that the crisp or thunderous word
Has been made flesh upon the screen,
The day's events a little blurred
Come to my ear. Ah, could it mean
Newscasters should be only heard,
Not seen?

REFLECTIONS ON THE FALLIBILITY OF PROGRESS

If all the world were Color
    From Rome to Roanoke,
No brighter and no duller
    Would sound the comic's joke;
If every screen, I figger,
    Stretched fifty inches down,
No smaller and no bigger
    The wit of any clown.

LAMENTS AND PRAISES

Dirge for an Era

O! do you remember Paper Books
   When paper books were thinner?
It was all so gay
In that far-off day
When you fetched them home
At a quarter a tome
   To dip in after dinner
Or carry to bed in a handy packet,
Bosomy girls on every jacket.
And never a taint of Culture
   Sullied that wholesome air
But only bodies
In Bishop's studies
   And blood on the bill-of-fare.
As the type grew blurry the plots grew thick.
But what do we get now?
Moby Dick.

Cluttering bookstore counters,
   In stationer's windows preening,
The Paperbacks
Now offer us facts
On Tillich and Sartre
And abstract artre
   And Life's essential Meaning,

Confessions by St. Augustine
   Instead of murderous men
Or many a yard
Of Kierkegaard
   And the myriad laws of Zen
Or books about bees and how they hive,
Cheap at a dollar-
Ninety-five.

You pack your trunk and you're at the station
But what do you find for a journey's ration?
Books by Aeschylus, books by Chaucer,
Books about atom or flying saucer,
Books of poetry, deep books, choice books,
Pre-Renaissance and neo-Joyce books,
In covers chaste and a prose unlurid.
Books that explore my id and *your* id,
Never hammock or summer-porch books
But Compass, Evergreen, Anchor, Torch Books,
Books by a thousand stylish names
And everywhere, everywhere, Henry James.

O! *do* you remember Paper Books
   When paper books were thrilling,
When something to read
Was seldom Gide
Or Proust or Peacock
Or Margaret Mead
   And seldom Lionel Trilling?
Gone is the sleuth that cheered our youth
   And the prose that galloped pure.
The flame of our pleasure burns to ash
Since shops are swept of their darling trash
And all we can buy for petty cash
   Is paper Literature.

Sunday Psalm

This is the day which the Lord hath made,
  Shining like Eden absolved of sin,
Three parts glitter to one part shade:
  Let us be glad and rejoice therein.

Everything's scoured brighter than metal.
  Everything sparkles as pure as glass—
The leaf on the poplar, the zinnia's petal,
  The wing of the bird, and the blade of the grass.

All, all is luster. The glossy harbor
  Dazzles the gulls that, gleaming, fly.
Glimmers the wasp on the grape in the arbor.
  Glisten the clouds in the polished sky.

Tonight—tomorrow—the leaf will fade,
  The waters tarnish, the dark begin.
But *this is the day which the Lord hath made:*
  Let us be glad and rejoice therein.

The Bonus

Of the small gifts of heaven,
It seems to me a more than equal share
At birth was given
To girls with curly hair.
Oh, better than being born with a silver ladle,
Or even with a caul on,
Is wearing ringlets sweetly from the cradle.
Slaves to no beauty salon,
Ladies whose locks grow prettier when moister
Can call the world their oyster.

Ladies with curly hair
Have time to spare.

Beneath a windy drier
They need not thumb through *Photoplay* each week.
They can look higher.
Efficient, tidy, and forever chic,
They own free hours to cook or study Greek,
Run for the Senate, answer notes, break par,
Write poems, chair the local D.A.R.,
Paint,
Or practice for a saint.

Ladies with curls are kind, being confident.
In smiles their lives are spent,
Primrosed their path.
Rising, like Venus, crinkly from the bath,
They keep appointments, punctual to the dot,
And do good works a lot.
In crises they are cool. 'Mid floods or wrecks,
Examples to their sex,
Steadfast they stand,
Calm in the knowledge not a hapless strand
Of hair is straggling down the backs of their necks.

However brief their lashes, plump their ankles,
The matter never rankles.
They marry well, are favorites with their kin.
Untyrannized by net and bobby pin,
They seldom cry "Alas!"
Or wring their hands or need divorce attorneys.
They are the girls boys choose at dancing class,
And they are beautiful on motor journeys.

Ah, pity her, however rose-and-white,
Who goes to bed at night
In clamps and clips!
Hers is no face to lure a thousand ships.
Had she been born unwavy,
Not Helen herself could ever have launched a navy.

Love Note to a Playwright

Perhaps the literary man
    I most admire among my betters
Is Richard Brinsley Sheridan,
    Who, viewing life as more than letters,
Persisted, like a stubborn Gael,
In not acknowledging his mail.

They say he hardly ever penned
    A proper "Yrs. received & noted,"
But spent what time he had to spend
    Shaping the law that England voted,
Or calling, on his comic flute,
The tune for Captain Absolute.

Though chief of the prodigious wits
    That Georgian taverns set to bubblin',
He did not answer Please Remits
    Or scoldings from his aunts in Dublin
Or birthday messages or half
The notes that begged an autograph.

I hear it sent his household wild—
    Became a sort of parlor fable—
The way that correspondence piled,
    Mountainous, on his writing table,
While he ignored the double ring
And wouldn't answer *any*thing;

Not scrawls from friends or screeds from foes
    Or scribble from the quibble-lover
Or chits beginning "I enclose
    Manuscript under separate cover,"
Or cards from people off on journeys,
Or formal statements from attorneys.

The post came in. He let it lie.
    (All this biographers agree on.)

Especially he did not reply
   To things that had R.S.V.P. on.
Sometimes for months he dropped no lines
To dear ones, or sent Valentines;

But, polishing a second act
   Or coaxing kings to license Freedom,
Let his epistles wait. In fact,
   They say he didn't even read'm.
The which, some mornings, seems to me
A glorious blow for Liberty.

Brave Celt! Although one must deplore
   His manners, and with reason ample,
How bright from duty's other shore,
   This moment, seems his bold example!
And would I owned in equal balance
His courage (and, of course, his talents),

Who, using up his mail to start
   An autumn fire or chink a crevice,
Cried, "Letters longer are than art,
   But *vita* is extremely *brevis!*"
Then, choosing what was worth the candle,
Sat down and wrote *The School for Scandal*.

Saturday Storm

This flooded morning is no time to be
Abroad on any business of mankind.
The rain has lost its casual charity;
It falls and falls and falls and would not mind
Were all the world washed blind.

No creature out of doors goes weatherproof.
Birds cower in their nests. The beast that can
Has found himself a roof.
This hour's for man

To waken late in, putter by his fire,
Leaf through old books or tear old letters up,
Mend household things with bits of thrifty wire,
Refill his coffee cup,
And, thus enclosed in comfort like a shell,
Give thought to, wish them well
Who must this day
On customary errands take their way:

The glistening policemen in the street,
For instance, blowing their whistles through the welter
And stamping their wet feet;
And grocery boys flung in and out of shelter
But faithful to their loads;
And people changing tires beside the roads;
Doormen with colds and doctors in damp suits;
And milkmen on their routes,
Scuttling like squirrels; and men with cleated boots
Aloft on telephone poles in the rough gale;
But chiefly trudging men with sacks of mail
Slung over shoulder,
Who slog from door to door and cannot rest
Till they've delivered the last government folder,
The final scribbled postcard, misaddressed.

Oh, all at ease
Should say a prayer for these—
That they come, healthy, homeward before night,
Safer than beasts or birds,
To no dark welcome but an earned delight
Of pleasant words,
Known walls, accustomed love, fires burning steady,
And a good dinner ready.

Song of High Cuisine

Written upon reading in the New York Times *that Bloomingdale's
grocery department now offers stuffed larks from the region of Carcassonne as well as one thrush from the French Alps.*

At Bloomingdale's,
At Bloomingdale's,
 Who would not wish to be—
Where hornèd are the Gallic snails,
 Where curls the anchovy!
For palate stales as winter fails
 And rainy spring comes on.
So they have birds at Bloomingdale's
 That flew in Carcassonne.

Yes, hark!
The lark
At heaven's gate,
 That lately sang so pure,
There trussed and truffled for the plate
 Invites the epicure.
And, sheltering from the Alpine wind
 In more than Alpine hush,
Arrives most elegantly tinned
 A solitary thrush.

Ah, few the sales
At Bloomingdale's,
 Amid imported straw,
Of tongues of foreign nightingales
 Or pearls in Malaga.
But they have many a merry thing.
 So who'll go there to buy
The little larks with parsleyed wing
That speak so eloquent of spring,
The single thrush that does not sing?

 Well, gentlemen, not I.

Eros in the Kitchen

Our cook is in love. Love hangs on the house like a mist.
It embraces us all.
The spoons go uncounted. Confused is the grocery list,
But light each footfall.
Astonished, we notice how lyric the dishwasher sings.
(Did it always sing thus?)
And the mop has a lilt. And the telephone ceaselessly rings,
Although seldom for us.
Here nothing seems quite the same as it did before.
Something ineffably hovers
Over the household. All of us plunge or soar
With the mood of the lovers.
We dine to distraction on delicate viands today
Who, likely, tomorrow
Must scrabble with timorous forks at a fallen soufflé
More sodden than sorrow.
And salad's served up with dessert and the napkin's forgot,
The butter's unformed by the mold,
And the bouillon's barbarically cold,
Or the aspic comes hot.
And the message for Mister or Madam's a fortnight untold.

But who's such a churl as to care
With amour like a mist on the air,
On the house like a bloom—
When so blithe is the broom,
And the voice of the kettle, the beat of the brush on the tile
Sound gayer than springtime peeper?
We smile at each other at breakfast. At dinner we smile.
There's a smile on the face of the sleeper.
Our years have grown younger. We sally to parties at night
In tall hat and long glove.
We remember what we had forgotten. The hallways are bright.
Our cook is in love.

Praise for an Institution

Of all museums,
I've a pet museum,
And it's not the Morgan
Or the Met Museum,
Or the Frick Museum,
Which steals the heart,
Or a trick museum
Like the Modern Art.
I must confess
It's a queer museum,
A more or less
Done-by-ear museum,
But it suits my nature
As knife suits fork:
The Museum of the City of New York.

A bit like an auction,
A bit like a fair,
Everything is cozy that's collected there.
Everything is cheerful as a Currier & Ives:
Capes made for gentlemen,
Caps for their wives;
Lamps lit at dark
By Great-Grandmama;
Central Park
In a diorama
(Where boys are sledding
And their runners curl);
A brownstone wedding
With a flower girl;
Doll-house parlors with carpet on the floor;
Patriotic posters from the First World War;
A solitary spur
That belonged to Aaron Burr;
And a small-scale model
Of a ten-cent store.

There for the dawdler,
Yesterday is spread—
Toys that a toddler
Carried once to bed;
Hoopskirts, horsecars,
Flags aplenty;
Somebody's dance dress, circa '20;
Somebody's platter, somebody's urn;
Mr. and Mrs.
Isaac Stern—
All gaily jumbled
So it's automatic
To believe you've stumbled
On your great-aunt's attic.
Helter-skelter
But large as life,
A room by Belter
And a room by Phyfe;
A period spinet,
A period speller;
The rooms that soured Mr. Rockefeller;
Rooms you can stare at, rooms you can poke in,
And a tenderhearted lobby
You can even smoke in.

It's a fine museum,
Not a new museum,
But a neighborly
Sort of old-shoe museum,
Not a class museum
Where the pundits go
Or a mass museum
With a Sunday show,
Not vast and grand
Like the Natural History.
How it ever got planned
Is a minor mystery.

But it fits my fancy
Like applesauce and pork,
The Museum of the City of New York.

The Sea Chantey Around Us

How vast, how clean
    The ageless ocean!
Whether serene
    Or in commotion,
Haunted by gull
    Or dolphin set.
How beautiful,
    How wild and wet!

Though rich and rare
    Its fauna and flora,
No evening's there
    And no aurora;
Instead, I think,
    A great supply
Of pearls and ink-
    Y octopi.

From pole to pole
    What whales take cover in,
The moon its sole
    Capricious sovereign,
Speaking in thunders
    Through its sleep,
Ah, rife with wonders
    Is the deep!

The waters tell it,
The billows shout it.
And I'm fed to the teeth with books about it.

The Forgotten Woman

Who are the friends of Dr. Gallup? Who,
Ah, who are they
Incessantly he puts inquiries to—
The ones who say
Their public yea or nay
On every matter controversy flares in?

Who fills those questionnaires in?

Where lurk the people Mr. Roper's minions
Implore for their opinions?
What straws define the wind, however it blows?
God knows.
All I can vouch for is the fact I see:
Nobody quizzes *me*.

Day after day across this mighty land,
While thunderous presses roll,
Young men with hats and briefcases in hand
(Or so I understand)
Wander from poll to poll,
Asking odd men in some peculiar street
Which candidate is theirs, which breakfast food
They least dislike to eat,
Which heresy offends their current mood.
But, left or right though thick the issues fall,
Nobody asks me anything at all.

Although I hold opinions firm and ample,
Unmatched as clues,
Nobody begs me will I be his Sample.
None wants my views—
Not even Fotographers from the *Daily News*.

Never do wheedling voices at my door
Ask how I stand on Nembutal for naps,

Or Christian soldiers marching off to war,
Or love, or coonskin caps,
Which virtue I prefer, which cigarette.
I never get
Called to the phone by females I'm no kin to
To say which TV program I'm tuned in to.

The counters and the checkers pass me by.
Ignored am I
Alike by those who augur, for a stipend,
Just how the votes have ripened
And by distinguished *Time*men gathering data
On everybody else's Alma Mata.

Still, hope's eternal. Here I stand and wait,
All needles-y and pins-y,
Thinking perhaps yon stranger at my gate
May come from Dr. Kinsey;
Might be, at worst, a messenger, delayed,
Seeking my choices for the Hit Parade.

But no one knocks to ask me, even now,
Am I detergent-minded or a soaper.
Where art thou, Gallup? Hooper, where art thou?
Where's Elmo Roper?
The breeze is freshening, the breeze is raw,
And here's your willing straw.
Before the unpolled generations trample me,
Won't *some*one sample me?

A Gallery of Elders

THE OLD FEMINIST

Snugly upon the equal heights
    Enthroned at last where she belongs,
She takes no pleasure in her Rights
    Who so enjoyed her Wrongs.

THE OLD PRELATE

God's House such decades has been his
    To tend, through fortune or disaster,
He half forgets now which he is—
    Custodian or Master.

THE OLD REFORMER

Few friends he kept that pleased his mind.
    His marriage failed when it began,
Who worked unceasing for mankind
    But loathed his fellow man.

THE OLD POLITICIAN

Toward caution all his lifetime bent,
    Straddler and compromiser, he
Becomes a Public Monument
    Through sheer longevity.

THE OLD RADICAL

The burning cause that lit his days
    When he was younger came to harm.
Now Hate's impoverished charcoal blaze
    Is all that keeps him warm.

THE OLD PHILANTHROPIST

His millions make museums bright;
    Harvard anticipates his will;
While his young typist weeps at night
    Over a druggist's bill.

THE OLD ACTOR

Too lined for Hamlet, on the whole;
    For tragic Lear, too coarsely built,
Himself becomes his favorite role,
    Played daily to the hilt.

THE OLD BEAUTY

Coquettes with doctors; hoards her breath
    For blandishments; fluffs out her hair;
And keeps her stubborn suitor, Death,
    Moping upon the stair.

June in the Suburbs

Not with a whimper but a roar
Of birth and bloom this month commences.
The wren's a gossip at her door.
Roses explode along the fences.

By day the chattering mowers cope
With grass decreed a final winner.
Darkness delays. The skipping rope
Twirls in the driveway after dinner.

Through lupine-lighted borders now
For winter bones Dalmatians forage.
Costly, the spray on apple bough.
The canvas chair comes out of storage;

And rose-red golfers dream of par,
And class-bound children loathe their labors,
While pilgrims, touring gardens, are
Cold to petunias of their neighbors.

Now from damp loafers nightly spills
The sand. Brides lodge their lists with Plummer.
And cooks devise on charcoal grills
The first burnt offerings of summer.

Reactionary Essay on Applied Science

I cannot love the Brothers Wright.
   Marconi wins my mixed devotion.
   Had no one yet discovered Flight
   Or set the air waves in commotion,
Life would, I think, have been as well.
That also goes for A. G. Bell.

What I'm really thankful for, when I'm cleaning up after lunch,
Is the invention of waxed paper.

That Edison improved my lot,
   I sometimes doubt; nor care a jitney
Whether the kettle steamed, or Watt,
   Or if the gin invented Whitney.
Better the world, I often feel,
Had nobody contrived the wheel.

On the other hand, I'm awfully indebted
To whoever it was dreamed up the elastic band.

Yes, pausing grateful, now and then,
   Upon my prim, domestic courses,
I offer praise to lesser men—
   Fultons unsung, anonymous Morses—
Whose deft and innocent devices
Pleasure my house with sweets and spices.

I give you, for instance, the fellow
Who first had the idea for Scotch Tape.

I hail the man who thought of soap,
   The chap responsible for zippers,
Sun lotion, the stamped envelope,
   And screens, and wading pools for nippers,
Venetian blinds of various classes,
And bobby pins and tinted glasses.

DeForest never thought up anything
So useful as a bobby pin.

Those baubles are the ones that keep
    Their places, and beget no trouble,
Incite no battles, stab no sleep,
    Reduce no villages to rubble,
Being primarily designed
By men of unambitious mind.

You remember how Orville Wright said his flying machine
Was going to outlaw war?

Let them on Archimedes dote
    Who like to hear the planet rattling.
I cannot cast a hearty vote
    For Galileo or for Gatling,
Preferring, of the Freaks of science,
The pygmies rather than the giants—

(And from experience being wary of
Greek geniuses bearing gifts)—

Deciding, on reflection calm,
    Mankind is better off with trifles:
With Band-Aid rather than the bomb,
    With safety match than safety rifles.
Let the earth fall or the earth spin!
A brave new world might well begin
With no invention
Worth the mention
Save paper towels and aspirin.

Remind me to call the repairman
About my big, new, automatically defrosting refrigerator with the
    built-in electric eye.

Season at the Shore

Oh, not by sun and not by cloud
And not by whippoorwill, crying loud,
And not by the pricking of my thumbs,
Do I know the way that the summer comes.
Yet here on this seagull-haunted strand,
Hers is an omen I understand—
Sand:

Sand on the beaches,
    Sand at the door,
Sand that screeches
    On the new-swept floor;
In the shower, sand for the foot to crunch on;
Sand in the sandwiches spread for luncheon;
Sand adhesive to son and sibling,
From wallet sifting, from pockets dribbling;
Sand by the beaker
    Nightly shed
From odious sneaker;
    Sand in bed;
Sahara always in my seaside shanty
Like the sand in the voice
Of J. Durante.

Winter is mittens, winter is gaiters
Steaming on various radiators.
Autumn is leaves that bog the broom.
Spring is mud in the living room
Or skates in places one scarcely planned.
But what is summer, her seal and hand?
Sand:

Sand in the closets,
    Sand on the stair,
Desert deposits
    In the parlor chair;

Sand in the halls like the halls of ocean;
Sand in the soap and the sun-tan lotion;
Stirred in the porridge, tossed in the greens,
Poured from the bottoms of rolled-up jeans;
   In the elmy street,
     On the lawny acre;
   Glued to the seat
     Of the Studebaker;
Wrapped in the folds of the *Wall Street Journal;*
Damp sand, dry sand,
Sand eternal.

When I shake my garments at the Lord's command,
What will I scatter in the Promised Land?
Sand.

The Spanish Lions

Guarding the doors of the Hispanic Society
At a Hundred and Fifty-fifth near Riverside,
Two lions sit, so charged with natural piety
(In the Virgilian sense), so filled with pride,
They seem less carved from rock than from the spirit
Of Spain. Oh, these are lords of the Spanish law,
Castilian lions, gilt-edged and eighteen-carat,
Hidalgos from rearing head to rigorous paw.

They are leaner than wasps. Yet neither thirst nor hunger
Possesses them. They thrive on honor alone,
Granite exemplars, as if when time was younger
All lions were haughty and Spanish and made of stone.
They look down their high-bred noses. Their manes are jaunty
As a matador's queue. They stare on nothing at all—
Not even the bas-relief of Rosinante,
Posed with his Knight astride, on the opposite wall.

PROPERTY OF
TRINIDAD HIGH
SCHOOL LIBRARY

Man with Pruning Shears

This gentleman loves all that grows—
    Bud, shoot, or bough that blossoms dapple.
He plants the rose and feeds the rose
    And guards the springtime apple;

Has a green thumb; is quick to praise
    The frailest petal in his borders;
Can heal (and with a myriad sprays)
    The peony's disorders.

So what has overtaken him,
    What frenzy set his wits to wander
That he should ravage limb by limb
    The wholesome lilac yonder?

That he should lay the privet low
    And do the vines such deadly treason
That scarce a twig, I think, will show
    Its leaf against this season?

A milder chap was never planned,
    Or one who dug with more decorum.
But now the weapon's in his hand,
    And branches thick before'm.

The selfsame madness takes his mind
    That took his mind when he was little
And owned a knife and could not find
    Sufficient sticks to whittle.

Apologia

When I and the world
Were greener and fitter,
Many a bitter
Stone I hurled.
Many a curse
I used to pitch
At the universe,
Being so rich
I had goods to spare;
Could afford to notice
The blight on the lotus,
The worm in the pear.

But needier grown
(If little wiser)
Now, like a miser,
All that I own
I celebrate
Shamefacedly—
The pear on my plate,
The fruit on my tree,
Though sour and small;
Give, willy-nilly,
Thanks for the lily,
Spot and all.

The Forties

THE WAR BEFORE THE LAST

The Portents

"Trial blackout of city studied by officials."
                    —*Headline in the* New York Times.

By a cloud, by rings on the moon
Or a bough that casts no shadow,
By the snowflake falling at noon
In a shriveled meadow
Do the knowing eye and the reason
Predict the season.

So who can regard the least
Of these things with pulse untroubled?
The wind has veered to the east,
The fields are stubbled,
And the shrewd airs inform
Us of the storm.

Whose hands—not yours, not mine—
Shall hold the floods in tether?
We have seen the cloud and the sign,
But we cannot stay the weather.
Run to your house. Pull fast
Your shutters on the blast.

Though there is no safety there,
I think. Nor anywhere.

Ballad of Fine Days

"Temperatures have soared to almost summer levels . . . making conditions ideal for bombing offensives."
—*Excerpt from B.B.C. news broadcast.*

All in the summery weather,
    To east and south and north,
The bombers fly together
    And the fighters squire them forth.

While the lilac bursts in flower
    And buttercups brim with gold,
Hour by lethal hour,
    Now fiercer buds unfold.

For the storms of springtime lessen,
    The meadow lures the bee,
And there blooms tonight in Essen
    What bloomed in Coventry.

All in the summery weather,
    Fleeter than swallows fare,
The bombers fly together
    Through the innocent air.

The Mixture as Before

Summer is icumen in,
    Sound the sirens, light the torches,
Warn the roses to begin
    Climbing up suburban porches.
Let the laurel run like fire
    Over all the upland reaches

But be wary of the wire,
   Barbed and bright, along the beaches.

Hark! The blithe, the morning bird,
   Early singing, stirs our slumber
Where the young man, undeferred,
   Waits upon his legal number.
Now the wren's unmortgaged nest
   Hugs our hospitable acre,
And the ski pole takes its rest
   With the rationed Studebaker.

Now the sails of summer fill,
   Now the waves are all a-glimmer,
Though attentive at his drill
   Stands the lean and sunburnt swimmer.
Now the lilies swoon with sun,
   Now the cricket pipes the shadows
And the anti-aircraft gun
   Crouches in astonished meadows.

Here is June. So let the ice
   Tinkle in unsweetened glasses.
Fling the immemorial rice.
   Strew the picnic on the grasses.
Tell the chattering mind to hush
   For one soft, deceptive hour
While the berry fires the bush
   And the bee invades the flower,

Till in lupine-colored light
   Dusk dissolves, the stars are certain,
And the aromatic night
   Leans against the blackout curtain.

Landscape Without Figures

The shape of the summer has not changed at all.
    There is no difference in the sky's rich color,
In texture of cloud or leaf or languid hill.
    The fringed wave is no duller.

Even the look of this village does not change—
    Shady and full of gardens and near the sea.
But something is lacking. Something sad and strange
    Troubles the memory.

Where are they?—the boys, not children and not men,
    In polo shirts or jeans or autographed blazers,
With voices suddenly deep, and proud on each chin
    The mark of new razors.

They were workers or players, but always the town was theirs.
    They wiped your windshield, they manned the parking lots.
They delivered your groceries. They drove incredible cars
    As if they were chariots.

They were the lifeguards, self-conscious, with little whistles.
    They owned the tennis courts and the Saturday dances.
They were barbarous-dark with sun. They were vain of their muscles
    And the girls' glances.

They boasted, and swam, and lounged at the drugstore's portal.
    They sailed their boats and carried new records down.
They never took thought but that they were immortal,
    And neither did the town.

But now they are gone like leaves, like leaves in the fall,
Though the shape of the summer has not changed at all.

Soldier Asleep

Soldier asleep, and stirring in your sleep,
In tent, trench, dugout, foxhole, or swampy slough,
I pray the Lord your rifle and soul to keep,
And your body, too,

From the hid sniper in the leafy tangle,
From shrapnel, from the barbed and merciless wire,
From tank, from bomb, from the booby trap in the jungle,
From water, from fire.

It was an evil wind that blew you hither,
Soldier, to this strange bed—
A tempest brewed from the world's malignant weather.

Safe may you sleep, instead,
Once more in the room with the pennants tacked on the wall,
Or the room in the bachelor apartment, 17 L,
The club room, the furnished room across the hall,
The room in the cheap hotel,

The double-decker at home, the bench in the park,
The attic cot, the hammock under the willow,
Or the wide bed in the remembered dark
With the belovèd's head beside you on the pillow.

Safe may the winds return you to the place
That, howsoever it was, was better than this.

Dido of Tunisia

I had heard of these things before—of chariots rumbling
    Through desolate streets, of the battle cries and the danger,
And the flames rising up, and the walls of the houses crumbling.
    It was told to me by a stranger.

But it was for love of the fair and long-robed Helen,
    The stranger said (his name still troubles my sleep),
That they came to the windy town he used to dwell in,
    Over the wine-dark deep.

In the hollow ships they came, though the cost was dear.
    And the towers toppled, the heroes were slain without pity.
But whose white arms have beckoned these armies here
    To trample my wasted city?

Ah, this, Aeneas, you did not tell me of:
That men might struggle and fall, and not for love.

Valedictorian

HIGH SCHOOL—1943

Stand up, young man with the pink and earnest face,
Tonight grown paler.
The crease of your new flannels pinch into place,
Tug at your collar.

The Principal, beaming parentward, has left the stand,
Having given his Message, complete with whimsical comment.
Stand up, my boy. Clutch the notes tight in your hand.
This is the eloquent moment.

On behalf of the Class, for yourself, for the monitors with
    their badges,
You have much to say.
Make the good-bys, make the promises and the pledges,
Map out the way.

Never farewells like yours were spoken before,
Against this shabby and familiar curtain.
Never was any future so naked and sure,
Or any path so certain.

There was always in other years a sound that was hollow
To the adolescent vow.
There were always the climbers and those who could not
    follow.
You will march together now.

One flashing destiny awaits you all:
Neither the job at the mill (or the drugstore counter)
Nor the wide campus colored with the fall
Nor the poolroom's banter.

There will be none left idling at the gate,
No prizes for the bolder,
But only the rifle resting its equal weight
On every shoulder.

So stand up, boy, forgetting the Golden Fleece.
Step to the rostrum, bow, and speak your piece.
There were never farewells spoken so stoutly here
Nor a path that showed so clear.

Ballad of Citations

"King George VI has knighted Lt. Gen. Mark W. Clark and Maj. Gen.
Walter Bedell Smith . . . and has awarded the order of Companion of
*t*ʰᵉ *Bath to Lt. Gen. George S. Patton."*
— *News item in the* New York World-Telegram.

"Hark, hark,"
Said General Clark,
    "Sir Mark is what I hight me."
Said General Smith
To his kin and kith,
    "The king was kind to knight me."
Then up rose General Patton,
    Who follows the iron path,
And "Fellows," he cried, "it's plain to see
You haven't heard how they've honored *me*.
For I'm Lieutenant General P.,
    Companion of the Bath!

"My voice may boom like a thunderclap,
    I'm tougher than Japs or Proosians,
But England claims I'm the proper chap
    To help with the royal ablutions—
To turn the tap and measure the tub
And fetch the brush for the royal scrub
    And see the floor has a mat on.
It isn't so much in the way of pelf,
And it's not the thing that I'd choose myself,
But—hand me those bath salts off the shelf,"
    Said General George S. Patton.

"Whoever I'm with,"
Spake General Smith,
    "They really must call me Sir now."
Yawned General Clark,
"When I stroll in the park,
    I cause a terrible stir now."

But General (Three-star) Patton,
   He turned from his guns to growl,
"Would either of you have the wit to cope
With the kingly sponge and the kingly soap
(The lavender or the heliotrope)?
   Could you marshal the kingly towel?

"The enemy fears my baleful eye,
   The foe abhors my power,
But Albion asks that I stand by
   When a monarch's in his shower.
Yes, I'm the man by the realm marked down
To handle the royal dressing gown.
   And this you can go to bat on—
Whenever I hear that bathroom bell,
I'll do my job and I'll do it well.
Though war, you'll have to admit, is h--l,"
   Said General George S. Patton.

On Every Front

Sickened by sounds of war and pillage,
   Wearied by rumors on the air
Of stricken town and wasted village
   And death and battle everywhere,
I fled the house that horror grew in,
I fled the wireless shouting ruin,
   To walk alone, a hopeful comer,
   In my green garden, ripe with summer.

I leaned my head above the rose
And while I watched, her natural foes—
Beetle and slug—in barbarous fettle,
Crept to consume her, leaf and petal.
I saw the ants amid the grass
   In foraging battalions pass,
Driving toward their disputed goal
For loot and *Lebensraum*. The mole,

Devious, secret, like a virus,
Bored from within upon the iris.

In captured trees had flung their tents
The caterpillar regiments.
Snails went in armor, scared and chilly,
While forward moved upon the lily
The cutthroat worm; but not for long.
Checking his desultory song,
A robin pulled the raider back
With one swift aerial attack,
But to be routed in disorder
By Tabby, pouncing from a border.

In bloody dust those armies weltered.
    Horde marched upon belligerent horde.
It was not peace my garden sheltered
    But the insatiable sword.
And watching there, I sighed. But soon,
On that same summer afternoon,
I took up arms and, stoutly met,
Slew twenty slugs with no regret.

Horrors of War

Upon this meek civilian head
    There fall few blows I can't put up with.
I slice my own unbuttered bread
    And creamless coffee fill my cup with.
To market in my rationed shoes
    I trudge on patient metatarsals,
Select the reds, tear out the blues,
    And homeward stagger with my parcels.
'Tis not the want of morning bacon,
    'Tis not the storage cupboard bare
Which cause my life at times to take on
    This aspect of despair.

It's amateur dietitians
Telling me how to make meat loaf out of peanut butter.

Should yet the government desire,
    I'll cast off wool and go in dimity,
My last, my lone, my ultimate tire
    Yield up with honest equanimity.
Each warden's rule, however slight,
    Finds my cooperation certain.
Obedient, at the fall of night
    I shade my lamp and draw my curtain.
Sweetly I pay the allotted fee
    (Per printed forms that thick and thin come)
On what I often laughingly
    Refer to as my income.

What depresses me is having to fill out all those little serial numbers
On all those little coupons.

For write this down in deathless crayon,
    These things are not the things that rankle:
The stocking made of vilest rayon
    Ignobly twisting round the ankle,
Suburban gardeners planning farms on
    The plots they scarce can turn a rake in,
The silly clocks without alarms on,
    The kitchen by the cook forsaken,
The butcher haughty in his den
    Dispensing curious chops, and thinner,
And never any extra men
    To ask for dinner.

Let the bomb burst, I shall not fear.
Let foemen march, I'll guard my city.
But none shall force this outraged ear
To listen to another radio crooner warbling another alleged patriotic
    ditty.

Admonition

To the Chicago Daily Times, *which is advocating a one-day smokers'*
fast to relieve the cigarette shortage.

Oh *Times,* oh reckless journal,
Oh sheet unblest!
What is this mischief, this design infernal
That you suggest?
Let smokers for one dreary day and night
Absent themselves, you say, from all delight.
Then we might see the secret stores unlocked,
The Luckies back, the shelves with Camels stocked.
Perhaps. I merely tender this advice:
Consider the Price.

Consider a nation
Biting its nails and wrestling with temptation
For twenty-four desperate hours.
Think of the tempers poised on murder's brink,
Of men at morning fainting in their showers,
Or driven, at eve, to drink.

Think, think
Of the vast quarrels let loose, the evil forces,
The words across the tables, the divorces,
Tots scurrying from the path
Of strange parental wrath,
Bosses, for once unwary,
Firing the blond and guiltless secretary,
Collaborations coming to an end,
Friend bickering with friend,
The innocent delivered to the furies
Of untobaccoed juries,
Deals lost, wives beaten, relatives told off,
And all for lack of a carload and a cough.

Through the small haze which wreathes about me yet
(From what now passes for a cigarette),
I conjure up the horrors of that day,
And, gentlemen, I say,
Resign your scheme. Quick, take your project back.
Better the lack,
The scramble, the shortage, the barley-flavored brand
Than anarchy across this smiling land.
Better, I cry, a bottleneck met head on
Than Armageddon.

Fiesta in the Reich

*"The German Propaganda Ministry last week warned the people not to
discuss military defeats and not to 'look depressed.'"*
—*News item in the* New York Times.

Come, lift a blithesome roundelay
    To wake the Seventh Sleeper.
The bomb is dropping from the bay,
    The Russ has crossed the Dnieper.
The Anglo-Saxon threatens Rome
    And perils every border.
But we'll be merry here at home
    By Goebbels' special order.
(Tra-la, tra-lay,
We're awfully gay,
    By brisk, official order.)

Though Liberators tour these skies
    So sacredly *der Führer's,*
We'll swear it's all a pack of lies
    Or maybe done with mührrors,

And dance and deck the streets with flowers
   Until our brows are beaded,
When told some new retreat of ours
   Has cleverly succeeded.
(We've made attack
By moving back,
   And brilliantly succeeded.)

The casual tear, the downcast look
   Are banned on edict simple.
We practice daily by the book
   To wear an *ersatz* dimple.
And if some fellow lost to shame,
   When friends break bread together,
Should call the future by its name,
   We talk about the weather. . . .
(Report the dunce
Of course, at once,
   And then discuss the weather.)

Chant of the Optimistic Butcher

Oh, once I sang of the sirloin,
   Of hamburgers once sang I,
Or oft would boast
Of the prime rib roast,
   Unrationed and hanging high.
But now with unction akin to piety,
I hymn the meats that are called Variety:

Variety meats, variety meats,
Who will buy my variety meats?

Regard, dear Moddom, this rich array.
   I've kidneys and sweetbreads
Fresh today.

I've tongue (a sliver),
   I've shanks and shins,
I've liver aquiver
   With vitamins.
I've succulent parts
   Of a similar stripe.
I've heads and hearts
   And masses of tripe.
Stew 'em with herbs or simmer in wine,
Season, stir,
And go out to dine.

The chop has gone from the showcase,
   The bacon no more I slice,
And I seldom drape on
The duck, the capon
   A Saturday Special price.
So gladly now to my soul I grapple
An order of Philadelphia scrapple.

Variety meats, variety meats,
Who will buy my variety meats?

Moddom, dear Moddom, take a chance.
   They're highly regarded,
I hear, in France.
The color's queer
   And the taste is awful,
But everything here
   Is yours, and lawful.
Yes, merry as grigs,
   Come sound the tocsin.
I've knuckles of pigs
   And tails of oxen.
And if the prospect should leave you glum,
Cheer up, for the *Wurst*
Is yet to come.

I've a morsel of brains for occasional treats.
Won't somebody buy my variety meats?

A Reader's-Eye View of the War

Now sound the trumpets, beat the drums,
 Let joy be open-handed,
For hail, the conquering hero comes,
 His brow with garlands banded.
He bears the marks of battles proud,
 Assorted honors grace him,
And who is first amid the crowd,
 Most fervent to embrace him?

His wife? His sire? The children four
 Whose features star his locket?
No, no! It is an Editor
 With contracts in his pocket.
And who, more tender than a spouse,
 His hand with rapture presses?
A scout, I think, from Random House
 Or maybe S. & S.'s.

Here come the valiant, here march the bold.
After them, Macmillan, e'er their deeds grow cold.
Home rolls the sailor, rescued from the brine;
Henry Holt will sign him on the signatory line.
Bring unholy ghosts, now, fetch the frantic quill.
The Publishers, the Publishers,
 Are crouching for the kill.

Upon some bloody field tonight
 Men breast the flood infernal,
For God, for Country, for the Right,
 And many a weekly journal.
No gunner at his smoking gun
 Lays down that grim utensil
But Mr. Luce is on the run
 To furnish him a pencil.

The castaway upon his raft
  Is probably engrossed now,
Composing, neatly paragraphed,
  His saga for the *Post* now,
While paratroopers turn a phrase
  In perilous positions.
The paths of glory nowadays
  Lead on to twelve editions.

Back fly the bombardiers with medals on their hearts.
Read it all in Collier's, *complete in seven parts.*
Look *will have the story with pictures underneath.*
Uneasy lies the head, lads, that wears a laurel wreath.
Though you escape the bullet and live to see the day,
The Magazines, the Magazines,
Will have you for their prey.

V-Day

Savor the hour as it comes. Preserve it in amber.
    Instruct the mind to cherish its sound and its shape.
Cut out the newspaper clippings. Forever remember
    The horns and the ticker tape,

The flags, the parades, the radio talking and talking,
    Ceaselessly crying the tale on the noisy air
(But omitting for once the commercials), the sirens shrieking,
    The bulletins in Times Square,

The women kneeling in churches, the people's laughter,
    The speeches, the rumors, the tumult loud in the street.
Remember it shrewdly so you can say hereafter,
    "That moment was safe and sweet.

"Safe was the day and the world was safe for living,
    For Democracy, Liberty, all of the coin-bright names.
Were not the bomb bays empty, the tanks unmoving,
    The cities no more in flames?

"That was an island in time, secure and candid,
    When we seemed to walk in freedom as in the sun,
With a promise kept, with the dangers of battle ended,
    And the fearful perils of peace not yet begun."

Spring Comes to the Suburbs

Now green the larch; the hedges green,
  And early jonquils go a-begging.
The thoughtful man repairs his screen,
  The child emerges from his legging.

By daylight now, commuters come
  Homeward. The grackle, unimpeded,
Forsakes his charitable crumb
  To loot the lawn that's newly seeded.

Tulips are mocked for their display
  By periwinkles' self-effacement,
And benedicts on ladders sway,
  Fetching the storm sash to the basement.

Still slumbers the lethargic bee,
  The rosebush keeps its winter tag on,
But hatless to the A & P
  The shopper rides in station wagon.

Once more Good Humor's wheedling bell
  Brings out the spendthrift in the miser,
And everywhere's the lovely smell
  Of showers and soil and fertilizer.

Ballroom Dancing Class

The little girls' frocks are frilly.
　The little boys' suits are blue.
On little gold chairs
They perch in pairs
　Awaiting their Friday cue.
The little boys stamp like ponies.
　The little girls coo like doves.
The little boys pummel their cronies
　With white, enormous gloves.
And overhead from a balcony
The twittering mothers crane to see.

Though sleek the curls
Of the little girls,
　Tossing their locks like foam,
Each little boy's tie
Has slipped awry
　And his hair forgets the comb.
He harks to the tuning fiddle
　With supercilious sneers.
His voice is cracked in the middle,
　Peculiar are his ears.
And little girls' mothers nod with poise
To distracted mothers of little boys.

Curtsying to the hostess,
　The little girls dip in line.
But hobbledehoy
Bobs each little boy,
　And a ramrod is his spine.
With little girls' charms prevailing,
　Why, as the music starts,
Are the little girls' mothers paling?
　And why do they clasp their hearts

When the hostess says with an arching glance,
"Let boys choose partners before we dance"?

Now little girls sway
Like buds in May
  And tremble upon the stalk.
But little boys wear
An arrogant air
  And they swagger when they walk.
The meagerest boy grows taller.
  The shyest one's done with doubt,
As he fingers a manful collar
  And singles his charmer out,
Or rakes the circle with narrowed eyes
To choose his suitable Friday prize.
While overhead in the balcony
The little boys' mothers smile to see
On razorless cheek and beardless chin
The Lord-of-Creation look begin.

Oh, little boys beckon, little girls bend!
And little boys' mothers condescend
(As they straighten their furs and pat their pearls)
To nod to the mothers of the little girls.

Reflections on the Daily Mail

For this, for this, Herodotus, despite
Snow, rain, or gloom of night,
Or cold that chills or tiger heat that parches,
Or predatory dog, or falling arches,
Some courier undismayed
(I'm quoting rather loosely from the Grecian)
Took his appointed round and was not stayed
Until its swift completion:

That I might find delivered to my door
A catalogue, a card
Announcing shantung selling by the yard
At something-eighty-four,
A notice that on Thursday I am due
For dental prophylaxis,
Two charity appeals, one copy of *Cue,*
A bill from Saks's.

The Tom-Tom

This is the day for bicycles.

Yesterday was a swimming day,
   A day for splashing head over heels,
When every child would have screamed dismay
At anything less than dolphin play.
   But today they are all on wheels.
Large and little and middle-sized,
An army of children goes mechanized.
As if for a silver medal,
Around and around they pedal.

And we saw no rockets fly,
   No messenger brought the word.
Yet lonely, lonely, the beaches lie
And the saltiest bathing suit is dry
While every child sweeps breathless by
   Like a bird, like a bird.
How did they know? What sign was sent
To herald the seashore's banishment?
Who proclaimed it the time and weather
For cycling all together?

Tomorrow, or the day after,
   The pedals will lose their power.

Solemn, and yet with laughter,
They will turn to something dafter,
   All at the selfsame hour.
All of a sudden the windy heights
Will burst into gaudy bloom of kites
   With a heaven-aspiring reach
   And a child attached to each.

But that hour overthrown,
   The falcon kites will be grounded.
As if a bugle had blown,
   As if a signal had sounded,
They will learn as one to be monster tall
When a madness of stilts assails them all.
Together in hot compliance,
They will walk the village like giants.

If you ask them, they are perplext.
   The calendar gives no warning.
One does not tell the next,
   Yet they wake and know in the morning
(As a swallow knows the time
   For quitting a rainy land),
When the rope should whirl to the skipping-rhyme
   Or the baseball thud in the hand,
Or the multitudinous din
Of the roller skates begin.

It is something that tom-toms say.
You cannot explain it away,
   Though reason or judgment reels.
For yesterday was a swimming day
And today is the same as yesterday,
   Yet now they are all on wheels.

I Know a Village

I know a village facing toward
　　Water less sullen than the sea's,
Where flickers get their bed and board
　　And all the streets are named for trees.

The streets are named for trees. They edge
　　Past random houses, safely fenced
With paling or with privet hedge
　　That bicycles can lean against.

And when the roots of maples heave
　　The solid pavements up that bound them,
Strollers on sidewalks give them leave
　　To thrust, and pick a way around them.

The little boats in harbor wear
　　Sails whiter than a summer wedding.
One fountain splashes in a Square.
　　In winter there's a hill for sledding;

While through October afternoons
　　Horse chestnuts dribble on the grass,
Prized above diamonds or doubloons
　　By miser children, shrill from class.

I know a village full of bees
　　And gardens lit by canna torches,
Where all the streets are named for trees
　　And people visit on their porches.

It looks haphazard to the shore.
　　Brown flickers build there. And I'd not
Willing, I think, exchange it for
　　Arcadia or Camelot.

Halloween

The night is moonstruck, the night is merry.
    Listen! It peals with a chime of words.
Twitters the town like an aviary,
    Haunted by voices stranger than birds'—
Haunted by shades abroad together,
    Shapes of childhood, mendicant ghosts,
Who claim the dark as their private weather,
    Walking the world in a giggling host.

They cast long shadows, or roly-poly.
    They tamper with doorbells. They chalk the stairs,
The night belongs to them, singly, wholly;
    Surer than Christmas this Feast is theirs.
Swarming past hedges like sparrows flocking,
    The gravel cracking beneath their feet,
Flutter the children. When they come knocking,
    Open the door to them, Trick or Treat.

Open the door to phantom and vagrant,
    Whistle them in from the wild outside,
For under the trees the leaves are fragrant,
    Over the houses the sky is wide,
And only a street lamp vaguely dapples
    Spellbound paths where the chestnut drops,
Comfort them quickly with candied apples.
    Stay them with pennies and lollypops.

Or they may forget how their beds are standing—
    Sheets turned down, and a light in the hall—
Forget the fire and the clock on the landing
    And never come back from the dark at all.
Coax them, wheedle them, call to them fonder
    Than ever you did on an evening yet,
For who knows whither a ghost may wander
    With mischief loose and the moon not set?
Treat them or trick them. But bar the door
Till the Shade is bewitched to a child once more.

Malediction

ON THE PEOPLE WHO HAVE BUILT A HOUSE
DIRECTLY ACROSS THE ROAD FROM OURS

Across our road there used to lie
    A little meadow, semirural,
Which seemed to a suburban eye
    View pleasanter than Alp or Ural.
Four birches grew there, leaning leeward,
And apple trees without a steward.

Day lilies lit an orange flame
    In June there. We could glimpse a steeple
And look on fields, until they came—
    This pair, these proud, presumptuous people,
With prints irrevocably blue
For a tall house to block our view.

They cut the meadow down alive,
    Cut down the leeward-leaning birches
To make the stylish cinder drive
    Where now their station wagon lurches.
Down went the lilies' yellow glory
And up their sordid second story.

Despiteful folk! With half earth's soil
    On which to rear their vile enclosure,
This single meadow must they spoil,
    The one that blest our south exposure.
But they shall rue the day they marred
The vista of an angry bard.

Confusion take their walls, their house!
    May termite dwell in porch and shutter;
In closet, moth; in pantry, mouse;
    And leaks in every copper gutter.
May they be haunted by disaster,
Including cracks in all the plaster.

Let rivers through their basement flow,
    Paint peel, pipes knock, screens fail in summer.
And may they call one fiend I know
    When, weekly, they must call a plumber.
Let tradesmen do them down in battle.
And may their midnight windows rattle.

My wrath on them across our lane
    Who laid those apples low with axes!
Come, smoking chimney, clogging drain,
    Drafts under doors, and higher taxes.
Come, swarm of wasp and plague of gnat;
Come, trouble with the thermostat;
Come, faithless eaves that buckle over;
Come, crab grass where was planted clover;
Come, dogs along their borders rooting!
And let them simply *loathe* commuting.

Perhaps that will instruct them to
Ravage a poet's favorite view!

Good Humor Man

Listen! It is the summer's self that ambles
    Through the green lanes with such a coaxing tongue
Not birds or daisy fields were ever symbols
    More proper to the time than this bell rung
With casual insistence—no, not swallow
    Circling the roof or bee in hollyhock.
His is the season's voice, and children follow,
    Panting, from every doorway down the block.

So, long ago, in some such shrill procession
    Perhaps the Hamelin children gave pursuit
To one who wore a red-and-yellow fashion
    Instead of white, but made upon his flute
The selfsame promise plain to every comer:
Unending sweets, imperishable summer.

Small-Town Parade

DECORATION DAY

Below the lawns and picket fences,
    Just past the firehouse, half a block,
Sharp at eleven-five commences
    This ardent and memorial walk
    (Announced, last night, for ten o'clock).

Solemn, beneath the elmy arches,
    Neighbor and next-door neighbor meet.
For half the village forward marches
    To the school band's uncertain beat,
    And half is lined along the street.

O the brave show! O twirling baton!
    O drummer stepping smartly out!
O mayor, perspiring, with no hat on!
    O nurses' aid! O martial rout
    Of Bluebird, Brownie, Eagle Scout!

And at the rear, aloof and splendid,
    Lugging the lanterns of their pride,
O the red firemen, well attended
    By boys on bicycles who ride
    With envious reverence at their side!

The morning smells of buds and grasses.
    Birds twitter louder than the flute.
And wives, as the procession passes,
    Wave plodding husbands wild salute
    From porches handy to the route.

Flags snap. And children, vaguely greeted,
    Wander into the ranks a while.

The band, bemused but undefeated,
    Plays Sousa, pedagogic style,
    Clean to the Square—a measured mile.

Until at last by streets grown stony,
    To the gray monument they bring
The wreath which is less testimony
    To Death than Life, continuing
Through this and every other spring.

Sonnets from the Suburbs

VILLAGE SPA

By scribbled names on walls, by telephone number,
    Cleft heart, bold slogan, carved in every booth,
This sanctum shall be known. This holy lumber
    Proclaims a temple dedicate to Youth.
Daily in garments lawful to their tribe,
    In moccasins and sweaters, come the Exalted
To lean on spotty counters and imbibe
    Their ritual Cokes or drink a chocolate malted.

This refuge is their own. Here the cracked voice,
    Giving the secret passwords, does not falter.
And here the monstrous deity of their choice
    Sits bellowing from his fantastic altar,
A juke-box god, enshrined and well at home,
    Dreadful with neon, shuddering with chrome.

P. T. A. TEA PARTY

The hats are flowered or the hats are furred
    According to the season. Plump and pretty,
Madam the Chairman says a plaintive word
    About the Milk-and-Midday-Lunch Committee.
The secretary, fumbling through her papers,
    Murmurs inaudibly the bleak returns

From Tuesday's Fun Fair. Someone lights the tapers
    Set, geometric, by the coffee urns.

Now from their chalky classrooms straggle in
    The apprehensive mentors of the young,
To be impaled like beetles on a pin
    By the sharp glance, the question-darting tongue
Of vested motherhood—while daylight droops
To smile and sip and talk of Hobby Groups.

SUBURBAN NEWSPAPER

Headlines, a little smudged, spell out the stories
    That stir the Friday village to its roots:
TOWN COUNCIL MEETS FOR MAY, MISS BABCOCK MARRIES,
    SHORE CLUB TO BAN BIKINI BATHING SUITS.
While elsewhere thunders roll or atoms shiver
    Or ultimate tyrants into dust are hurled,
Weekly small boys on bicycles deliver
    News to our doors of this more innocent world—

A capsule universe of church bazaars
    Where even the cross-stitched aprons sell on chances,
Of brush fires, births, receptions, soda bars,
    Memorial Day parades, and high-school dances,
And (though on various brinks the planet teeters)
Of fierce disputes concerned with parking meters.

COMMUNITY CHURCH

The Reverend Dr. Harcourt, folk agree,
    Nodding their heads in solid satisfaction,
Is just the man for this community.
    Tall, young, urbane, but capable of action,
He pleases where he serves. He marshals out
    The younger crowd, lacks trace of clerical unction,
Cheers the Kiwanis and the Eagle Scout,
    Is popular at every public function,

And in the pulpit eloquently speaks
    On divers matters with both wit and clarity:

Art, Education, God, the Early Greeks,
  Psychiatry, Saint Paul, true Christian charity,
Vestry repairs that shortly must begin—
  All things but Sin. He seldom mentions Sin.

OCCUPATION: HOUSEWIFE

Her health is good. She owns to forty-one,
  Keeps her hair bright by vegetable rinses,
Has two well-nourished children—daughter and son—
  Just now away at school. Her house, with chintzes
Expensively curtained, animates the caller.
  And she is fond of Early American glass
Stacked in an English breakfront somewhat taller
  Than her best friend's. Last year she took a class

In modern drama at the County Center.
  Twice, on Good Friday, she's heard *Parsifal* sung.
She often says she might have been a painter,
  Or maybe writer; but she married young.
She diets. And with Contract she delays
The encroaching desolation of her days.

LENDING LIBRARY

Between the valentines and birthday greetings
  With comical verses, midway of the aisle,
Here is a rendezvous, a place of meetings.
  Foregathers here the lady bibliophile.
A dollar down has bought her membership
  In this sorority. For three cents daily
Per paper-jacketed volume she can dip
  Deep in Frank Yerby or Miss Temple Bailey,

Lug home the current choices of the Guild
  (Commended by the press to flourish of trumpets),
Or rent a costume piece adroitly filled
  With goings on of Restoration strumpets—
And thus, well read, join in without arrears
The literary prattle of her peers.

BEAUTY PARLOR

The lady in Booth Three is discontented
   With her last wave, rejects the oil shampoo
As if it were a bribe. Ammonia-scented,
   The permanent begins in Number Two.
Five thinks perhaps she'd like to take a flyer
   On something upswept. Elderly Mrs. Sloane,
From Number Seven, deafened by the dryer,
   Confides abruptly in a public tone

To Miss Estelle the history of her spleen.
   Six orders sandwiches. The pages flutter,
On aproned laps, of *Look* and *Silver Screen*.
   Seven, alarmed, subsides now to a mutter,
And Three debates the problem whether to dapple
Her nails with Schoolhouse Red or Stolen Apple.

VOLUNTEER FIREMAN

Four strident whistles means the business section,
   Two longs and a short, the Manor; three, the Park.
He knows the signals vaguely. With direction
   He can unhook a ladder in the dark,
Rescue canaries, save a mattress whole
   Or pass the cups of coffee laced with brandy.
No midnight blaze but finds him ready to roll,
   Providing he's awake and the Buick handy.

Monthly he drills. But valor has its inning
   That autumn night when by an annual route,
Helmeted, gloved, with all the torches shining,
   He marches proudly in his crimson suit—
A boy of forty who has skimmed the cream
From childhood's first and most enduring dream.

COUNTRY CLUB SUNDAY

It is a beauteous morning, calm and free.
The fairways sparkle. Gleam the shaven grasses.
Mirth fills the locker rooms and, hastily,
    Stewards fetch ice, fresh towels, and extra glasses.
On terraces the sandaled women freshen
    Their lipstick; gather to gossip, poised and cool;
And the shrill adolescent takes possession,
    Plunging and splashing, of the swimming pool.

It is a beauteous morn, opinion grants.
    Nothing remains of last night's Summer Formal
Save palms and streamers and the wifely glance,
    Directed with more watchfulness than normal,
At listless mate who tugs his necktie loose,
Moans, shuns the light, and gulps tomato juice.

THE 5:32

She said, If tomorrow my world were torn in two,
Blacked out, dissolved, I think I would remember
(As if transfixed in unsurrendering amber)
This hour best of all the hours I knew:
When cars came backing into the shabby station,
Children scuffing the seats, and the women driving
With ribbons around their hair, and the trains arriving,
And the men getting off with tired but practiced motion.

Yes, I would remember my life like this, she said:
Autumn, the platform red with Virginia creeper,
And a man coming toward me, smiling, the evening paper
Under his arm, and his hat pushed back on his head;
And wood smoke lying like haze on the quiet town,
And dinner waiting, and the sun not yet gone down.

MODERN TIMES

Brief History of Modern Man

Tiptoe, the weathercock
Pursues his furious search
For pure Authority.
Upon his giddy perch
(More wavering than rock),
He postures, "Follow me!

"Here's Truth from the wind's mouth.
This is the final Weather,
Revealed for man or beast."
Then he and wind, together,
Pointing but lately south,
Whirl instantly to east.

Wind veers again. He goes,
With faith as firm as ever,
Around and 'round his route.
Feeling immensely clever,
He stretches on his toes
To tell the Absolute,

Proclaiming as he spins,
"The Truth is in the West.
Forget the old illusion."
So, at each gust, begins
His unavailing quest
That comes to no conclusion—
And comes to no conclusion.

Moody Reflections

When blithe to argument I come,
  Though armed with facts, and merry,
May Providence protect me from
  The fool as adversary,
Whose mind to him a kingdom is
  Where reason lacks dominion,
Who calls conviction prejudice
  And prejudice opinion.

Yes, when with dolts I disagree,
  Both *sic* and also *semper,*
May my good angels succor me
  And help me hold my temper.
But strength from what celestial store
  Shall keep my head from bending
When I behold whom I abhor—
The snob, the bigot, and the bore—
Wielding their witless cudgels for
  The cause that I'm defending?

The Town That Tries Men's Souls

*"Philadelphia—The Fairmount Park Commission refused permission
today for a statue of Tom Paine to be erected in the park on the ground
that "his writings indicated that he was an atheist."*
                              —News item in the New York Times.

I give you the City of Brotherly Love,
The home of the Blue Law, the haunt of the Dove,
Where the Liberty Bell in a showcase resides,
With dents in the clapper and cracks in the sides.
There Sunday's reserved for the spirit that droops,
There all of the houses have similar stoops,

And there on the greensward no hero may perch
Who didn't belong to an orthodox church.

For Philadelphia,
Philadelphia,
   Has Standards to maintain,
And they wouldn't care
To pollute the Square
   With a statue of Th-m-s Pa-ne.

Ah, think of the gossip and think of the scandal
To bell and to book and municipal candle!
Consider the shock to a village so cloistered,
Whose train is the Pennsy, whose taverns are oystered.
The cricket clubs shiver, the Main Line is trembly,
While débutantes pale at the gilded Assembly
Lest Thomas the Doubter and Thomas the Dark
Should dare to invade a respectable park.

O Philadelphia,
Philadelphia,
   Her virtue is pearled and rubious,
And she swerves no jot
For a patriot
   With background a trifle dubious.

For Tom might star on historical lists,
But he didn't confide in the Calvinists;
He wasn't a Baptist, he wasn't a Shaker,
He certainly wasn't an affluent Quaker.
Doubtless his sentiments pleased the Lord,
But he never sat on a vestry board;
He seldom quoted from Chapter and Verse,
He didn't sprinkle, he didn't immerse.
His words were food for a hungering nation,
But where's the letter from his congregation?

We mustn't encourage his like again
In the city founded by William Penn.

Home Is the Sailor

*Lines written upon hearing that inmates of Sailors Snug Harbor, an
institution with an estimated thirty-million-dollar endowment, have
been asked to sign over to the corporation all private income, including
pensions, savings, and social security monies.*

When sailors snug in harbor sit
    And munch the bread Endowment measures,
It is not meet, it is not fit,
    That they should yearn for grosser pleasures.

What can an old man want but sleep,
    Gossip, his pipe, the daily plateful,
And Institution rules to keep,
    And prompt advice on being grateful?

The private dollar in the purse,
    The treat that is not quite a rarity,
Could breed but discontent or worse—
    Would dull the cutting edge of Charity.

Give them the ancient's proper due:
    A bed, a bench, a wall that's sunny,
And immemorial truth to chew:
    Only the rich have need of money.

Note to My Neighbor

We might as well give up the fiction
    That we can argue any view.
For what in me is pure Conviction
    Is simple Prejudice in you.

Mourning's at Eight-Thirty

OR, A HEADLINE A DAY KEEPS EUPHORIA AWAY

'Tis day. I waken, full of cheer,
    And cast the nightmare's shackle.
Hark, hark! the sanguine lark I hear
    Or possibly the grackle.

Phoebus arises. So do I;
    Then, tuneful from the shower,
Descend with head and courage high
    To greet the breakfast hour.

All's well with all my world. I seem
    A mover and a shaper
Till from the doorstep with the cream
    I fetch the morning paper—

Till I fetch in the paper and my hopes begin to bleed.
There's a famine on the Danube, there's a crisis on the Tweed,
And the foes of peace are clever,
And my bonds no good whatever,
And I wish I had never
    Learned to read.

The coffee curdling in my cup
    Turns bitterer than tonic,
For stocks are down and steaks are up
    And planes are supersonic.

Crops fail. Trains crash. The outlook's bright
    For none except the coffiner,
While empires topple left and right,
    Though Leftward rather oftener,

And Russia will not come to terms,
    And Sikhs are full of passion,
And each advertisement affirms
    My wardrobe's out of fashion.

Oh, I see by the papers we are dying by degrees.
There's a war upon our border, there's a blight upon our trees;
And to match each Wonder Drug up
That our scientists have dug up,
They have also turned the bug up
 Of a painful new disease.

At eventide the journals face
 In happier directions.
They like a juicy murder case,
 They dote on comic sections.

But in the morning even "Books"
 Sends shudders coursing through me.
The outlook for the Drama looks
 Intolerably gloomy,

And though the sun with all his heart
 Is shining round my shoulder,
I notice by the weather chart
 Tomorrow will be colder.

Oh, I wake in the dawning and my dreams are rosy-red,
But the papers all assure me there's destruction straight ahead.
If the present's pretty dismal,
Why, the future's quite abysmal,
And I think that I'll just

 crawl

 back

 to

 bed.

Post-Election Ruminations

The tumult and the shouting dies.
    The Captains rally to their mutton,
And from lapel the voter pries
    His bright, identifying button.

Manned by a loud-exulting crew,
    The Ship of State is safely harbored
(Or else, according to one's view,
    Has sunk to leeward and to starboard).

Now lesser voices split the air,
    Crying their cosmic pills and nostrums;
Now droop the placards in the square,
    Now fades the bunting round the rostrums.

While friend with his dissenting friend
    Speaks once again, assured and hearty,
Finding the world has yet to end
    With victory for the Other Party—

That heaven stands, the sunset burns,
    Cheerful, accustomed, and eternal,
In spite of what the late returns
    Foreshadowed in an evening journal.

And on we stumble as before,
    Skirting somehow the black abyss,
Tough from a hundred years or more
    Of crises noisier than this.

The Chosen People

"The brunt [of the new tax] will be borne by the middle brackets."
—*News item from the* New York Times.

I'm a middle-bracket person with a middle-bracket spouse
And we live together gaily in a middle-bracket house.
We've a fair-to-middling family; we take the middle view;
So we're manna sent from heaven to Internal Revenue.

      We're the pride of every sector.
        We're the darlings of the land.
      To the income-tax collector
        We extend a helping hand.
      For the poor have empty pockets
        And the rich bewail the Day,
      But the middle-bracket patriots
        Are steady with their pay.

When there's duty to accomplish, it's our duty that we do.
Though the world is in a muddle, we contrive to muddle through.
We are first in all the battles as we're first in every peace,
And we lead the van devoutly when the levies must increase.

      The upper brackets, nightly,
        Have dreams of What's Beyond,
      And to their bosoms tightly
        They clutch the taxless bond.
      The cheerful lower brackets
        Get coupons from the gov.,
      But the people in the middle
        Own the legislature's love.

Oh, we reimburse the dentist and we meet the butcher bills.
We're the folk who keep the temples up, along the templed hills.
We are sturdy as to shoulder and our collars all are white.
So the income-tax department keeps us forming to the right.

Then sing a song of sixpence
    And ninety billions more.
Hum a ballad for the wolf
    That hangs about the door.
But chant a pretty ditty
    Until the welkin rings
For the middle-bracket citizens
    Who bear the brunt of things.

The Great Enigma

I hear that Mr. Morgenthau,
    Who sits in office, stately,
Has many a wrinkle in his brow
    Which was not there till lately,
From wondering how to solve aright
    This problem on his docket:
The money that is burning bright
    In everybody's pocket.
But though it's money, plain enough,
    That turns inflation's key,
What happens to the pretty stuff
    Before it gets to me?

> *The money, the money,*
> *It's surely very funny*
> *What happens to the money*
> *Before it reaches me.*

Now everyone is getting rich—
    The infant and his elder,
The digger in the union ditch,
    The merchant and the welder.
The miner climbs a golden ground,
    The jack a golden steeple,
But I don't seem to get around
    Among the proper people.

For faithful as the wolf who howls
    Along this private sector,
Beside my door, incessant, prowls
    The income-tax collector.
My salary dwindles when it's due,
    Exploding like a comet,
And every day there's something new
    To be deducted from it.

Yes, let each bureaucratic gent
    Improve the shining hour
Inventing plans to circumvent
    The nation's buying power,
And let him study in his cell
    How best to prick the bubble,
But as for me, he might as well
    Just save himself the trouble.
For farmers live on clotted cream,
    Machinists draw their pay,
But something dams the flowing stream
    Before it comes my way.

      The money, the money,
      That makes existence sunny!
      What happens to the money
      Before it comes my way?

Daniel at Breakfast

His paper propped against the electric toaster
    (Nicely adjusted to his morning use),
Daniel at breakfast studies world disaster
    And sips his orange juice.

The words dismay him. Headlines shrilly chatter
    Of famine, storm, death, pestilence, decay.
Daniel is gloomy, reaching for the butter.
    He shudders at the way

War stalks the planet still, and men know hunger,
   Go shelterless, betrayed, may perish soon.
The coffee's weak again. In sudden anger
   Daniel throws down his spoon

And broods a moment on the kitchen faucet
   The plumber mended, but has mended ill;
Recalls tomorrow means a dental visit,
   Laments the grocery bill.

Then, having shifted from his human shoulder
   The universal woe, he drains his cup,
Rebukes the weather (surely turning colder),
   Crumples his napkin up
And, kissing his wife abruptly at the door,
Stamps fiercely off to catch the 8:04.

Litany for the Unorganized

I want to belong to a Union
   And own a Union card
With time and half for overtime
   And benefits by the yard,
With a Union pin for my coat lapel
   And a Union scale of pay.
For the garrulous names of the A. F. of L.
   Keep haunting me night and day.

Do I hear a rousing welcome from the laborers of the nation?
   International Union of United Brewery, Cereal & Soft Drink
      Workers of America, are you with me to a man?
Will you have me for a member, Roofers, Damp & Waterproof
      Workers' Association?
   Or you, Union of Journeyman Horseshoers of United States &
      Can.?

Before my years turn colder
  And the days toward darkness press,
Oh, give me the card of a Molder
  Or a Special Delivery Mess.!
For the dues they weigh in my pocket,
  Ambition burns like flame,
And I want to dwell
In the A. F. of L.
  And wear a Union name.

Sheepshearers of North America, think lengthily and well on me.
  Union of Glass-Bottle Blowers, come give me your answer true,
For the sound of your teeming titles has cast a fatal spell on me.
  International Association of Marble, Slate & Stone Polishers,
    Rubbers & Sawyers, Tilers & Marble Setters, Helpers &
    Terrazzo Helpers, I love you.

Confessions of a Reluctant Optimist

When flaming comrades I admire
  (And in whose breasts was ever coddled
Dissatisfaction's honest fire)
  Argue how to their hearts' desire
    The universe should be remodeled—

When of their wrongs they call the roll,
  Vowing that fortune is a hellion,
Shamefaced I sit, an outcast soul,
  Incapable of true rebellion.

For, though aware that life is what
  One ought to view with wrath and gravity,
I live delighted with my lot,
  Sunk in content as in depravity.

Less woman, I expect, than mouse,
  To alter fate I would not bother.

I like my plain suburban house.
　　I like my children and their father.

Quite able to believe the decks
　　Are stacked for females—much it boots me!
I would not willing change my sex.
　　It is the very sex which suits me.

In fact, I find it hard to see
　　Exactly what I ought disparage.
I like my nationality,
　　I like my relatives-by-marriage.

Trapped, tricked, enslaved, but lacking sense
　　To enter in the conflict single,
I wear my chains like ornaments,
　　Convinced they make a charming jingle.

Alas, alack, how well I know
　　My kind's a drawback to the nation!
But here I am and here I go,
Contented with the status quo,
　　And quite beyond salvation.

Without a Cloak

Hate has a fashionable cut.
　　It is the garment man agrees on,
Snug, colorful, the proper weight
　　For comfort in an icy season.

And it is weatherproof, they say—
　　Becoming, also, to the spirit.
I fetched Hate homeward yesterday,
　　But there it hangs. I cannot wear it.

It is a dress that suits me ill,
　　However much the mode sustains me.

At once too ample and too small,
    It trips, bewilders, and confines me.

And in my blood do fevers flow,
    Corruptive, where the fabric presses,
Till I must pluck it off as though
    It were the burning shirt of Nessus.

Proud walk the people folded warm
    In Hate. They need not pray for spring.
But threadbare do I face the storm
    Or hug my hearthstone, shivering.

Ordeal in Hungary

With honest fire and simple flame
    To Orleans' maid they put the question.
It was a mortal arrow came
    To still the ardors of Sebastian.

Mild Thomas, welcoming the steel,
    By mercy's self was unforsaken
And Catherine upon her wheel
    Gave only body to be broken.

But man has flourished, has been quick
    To learn new arts of death and torment.
Now must the stubborn heretic
    Yield up the spirit with its garment.

Now he who wears compassion's face
    Or carries conscience for a banner
Must meet his captors, stripped of grace,
    Wit, reputation, will, and honor,

And suffer more outrageous loss,
    A martyrdom more fresh-discovered,
Than Andrew joyful on his cross
    Or Stephen to the stones delivered.

Incident in the Afternoon

I heard two ladies at a play—
　　A comedy considered witty.
It was a Wednesday matinée
　　And they had come from Garden City.
Their frocks were rather arts-and-crafts,
And they had lunched, I learned, at Schrafft's.

Although we did not speak or bow
　　Or comment even on the weather,
More intimate I know them now
　　Than if we'd gone to school together.
(As you must presently divine,
Their seats were rather near to mine.)

Before the curtain rose I heard
　　What each had told her spouse that morning.
I learned the history, word for word,
　　Of why three cooks had given warning.
Also that neither cared a straw
For domineering sons-in-law.

I heard a bridge hand, play by play.
　　I heard how all's not gold that glitters.
I heard a moral résumé
　　Of half a dozen baby-sitters.
I learned beyond the slightest question
Shrimps are a trial to digestion.

The lights went down. The stage was set.
   Still, in the dusk that fans the senses,
Those ladies I had never met
   Poured out their swollen confidences.
The dialogue was smart. It stirred them
To conversation. And I heard them.

Above each stylish epigram
   Wherewith the hero mocked his rival,
They proved how nicely curried lamb
   Might justify a roast's revival,
That some best-selling author's recent
Book was lively. But indecent.

I heard a list of maladies
   Their all too solid flesh was heir to.
I heard that one, in her deep freeze,
   Could store a steer, but did not care to.
A neighbor's delicate condition
I heard of, all through intermission.

They laid their lives, like open tomes,
   Upon my lap and turned the pages.
I heard their taste in hats and homes,
   Their politics, but not their ages.
So much I heard of strange and true
Almost it reconciled me to
One fact, unseemly to recall:
I did not hear the play at all.

Raddled Rhyme in Praise of Poodles

Sealyhams waddle,
    Newfoundlands cuddle,
Airdales all dawdle
    On corners to grouse.
Dachshunds know oodles
    Of reasons to huddle.
But Poodles
            Walk proud in the house.

Boxers are addled
    With love. They speak twaddle;
Guests are bestraddled,
    Kissed, pummeled, embraced.
Cockers have noodles
    Enchanting to model.
But Poodles
            Have manners and taste.

Needless and idle
    On Poodle, the paddle.
Learning's a bridle
    He's panting to wear.
Ruffed to the middle,
    He'll sit or skedaddle,
Play fiddle,
            Or waltz to an air.

Collie's a breed'll
    Guard babes in the cradle;
Springers can wheedle
    A bird from a tree.
Dobermans muddle,
Pugs scorn a puddle,
Beagles can yodel,
Though slightly off key.

Scotties win medals,
Pekinese toddle,
Chows, while a riddle,
Are tempting to coddle.
Yet, kit and caboodle,
No peer has the Poodle.
For Poodle
           Thinks highly of Me.

Hostess

Her delicate hands among the demitasses
Flutter like birds.
She smiles, and from her smiling mouth releases
A shower of words
Shrewdly designed to set
The dust of any private tête-à-tête.

Now, having drained the ceremonial cup,
Let none expect her pardon
But every guest fanatically take up
The evening's burden,
Answer the roll of names
And spring with quick obedience to the Games.

Let every voice grow shrill, let laughter rise.
He who has fed must caper.
She prowls the drawing room with watchful eyes,
Filling the glasses, passing the slips of paper,
And desperately bent
On stirring up a scheduled merriment.

No calm must fall, however brief and narrow,
Lest to her dread,
From some small knothole of silence, some hidden burrow,
The scotched snake, Thought, should rear its venomed head.

Notes Written on a Damp Veranda

Do they need any rain
In Portland, Maine?
  Does Texas pray for torrents,
The water supply
Run dry, run dry,
  From the ancient wells of Florence?
Is the vintage grape
In perilous shape
  On the slopes of Burgundy?
Let none despair
At the arid air—
  They've only to send for me.
Invite me to stay for a holiday
  And the rain will follow me.

Rain is my lover, my apple strudel.
It haunts my heels like a pedigreed poodle.
Beyond the seas or across the nation,
It follows me faithful on every vacation.

Others back from Bermuda wander
Burning pink as an oleander.
But sun turns off like a Macy gadget
The minute I set a foot in Paget.

It rains when I go to a Brookline wedding.
Friday to Monday it rains in Redding.
All that I've seen of a bay called Oyster
Is part of the ocean getting moister.

The tops of umbrellas was all I saw,
The time I attended the Mardi Gras.
And it hadn't rained for a year in Tucson
Till I was the guest the clouds let loose on.

Wherever I travel, wherever I hie,
Tumult begins in the cumuli,

The mold creeps over the pillow's feather,
And flaps of envelopes stick together.

I never land
With my bags in hand
   But floods inspire the greenery.
I bring fresh showers
For the thirsting flowers
   But I don't see much of the scenery.
The desert's a rose where I am, God knows,
   But I don't see much of the scenery.

So Noah was lucky, I guess, at that,
I wasn't weekending on Ararat.

Honest Confession

The things are three
   Which I discern
Less easily
   As the years turn.

Three things seem sliding
   From my sight:
The line dividing
   Wrong from right;

Whereto we hie
   From where we've been to;
The needle's eye
   A thread goes into.

Death at Twilight

Verses composed upon hearing that scientists are recording the mating calls of mosquitoes and plan to use them to lure the insects to their downfall.

When summer's warm upon the breeze
    And evening shrouds the glens,
Oh, pity poor Anopheles
    And Culex Pipiens,
Whom Science, on deliberate vote,
Has destined for a *Liebestod.*

The mists will fall, the moon will rise,
    Darkness the daylight veto.
Then forward to his strange demise
    Will race the blithe mosquito,
Antennae tuned to catch the tender
Accents of the female gender.

From duty will he turn away
    To bear an ardent torch.
He'll leave his work and leave his play
    On patio or porch,
Desert the foray intramural,
The city roof, the terrace rural,
The chosen grasses, moist and deep,
The chamber dedicate to sleep,
The bright, the unscreened living room,
And hurry off to meet his doom—
Yea, quit, no matter how it rankles,
His job on easy arms and ankles.

Forgoing much, forgetting all,
    Save love or matrimony,
He'll fly—to find that mating call
    A trick, a trap, a phony,

And come to grief with no defense,
The victim of his sentiments.

For thus, weighed down by nature's fetters,
The lower orders ape their betters.

Reflections on a Dark Day

Now and then there seems some doubt
I have much to brag about.
Cleo, serpent of the Nile,
Owned a more romantic style,
Mary upped more Scottish bonnets,
Laura won diviner sonnets,
Saint Theresa's soul was sunnier,
Austen wrote a good deal funnier,
Braver far was Molly Pitcher,
Even Hetty Green got richer.

Now and then I tell my mirror:
Isolde's lovers held her dearer,
Joan was better versed in miracle,
Sappho's poems read more lyrical,
Staël attracted people wittier,
Jenny Lind could carol prettier,
And it's plain that Helen's powers
Burnt a lot more topless towers.
Still and all, there's this I've got—
They are dead and I am not.

A Choice of Weapons

Sticks and stones are hard on bones.
Aimed with angry art,
Words can sting like anything.
But silence breaks the heart.

Monologue in a Pet Shop

Some folk discourse
On the noble horse
   And some by newts are smitten,
While others aver
Their heartstrings stir
   At sight of a frolic kitten.
For every brute,
Though meek, though mute,
   There's somebody madly cares,
But me, I think
I'll settle for mink
   Done up by Revillon Frères.

For I am a lady with pet resistance.
Now, take the dog (and to any distance).
He's a faithful buddy
   To man, no doubt,
But his paws are muddy,
   His hair falls out.
In accents florid
   At dawn he rehearses.
His bark is horrid,
   His bite much worse is.
At little dangers
   He crawls away closer.
He follows strangers
   But nips the grocer.
You fondle, you feed him,
   You guard his habits.
And when you need him,
   He's chasing rabbits.

I lift my lute and I tune my lyre
In bold defiance of Ellin Speyer.
For cats are clawers,
   Their blood runs clammily,

In bureau drawers
  They deposit their family.
Horses are splendid
  As things to bet on,
But not intended
  For me to get on.
Goldfish stare at one,
  Calm and chilly.
Parrots swear at one,
  Monkeys act silly.
Mice I'm at bay from.
  Birds are a bore.
Pets, keep away from
  My cottage door.

It's true the acumen
Of Genus human
  Is lower than spire or steeple,
But the more I see
Of the Pekinee,
  The more I am fond of people.

Report on a Situation

Tears at midnight
  Stain the pillow
Tears at morning
  Puff the eye.
Twilight tears are
  Brief and shallow—
Easy-summoned,
  Quick to dry.
Saltier sting those tears, they say,
  Never shed by night or day.

Song for a Personal Prejudice

January's bearable
In spite of bad report.
Though February's terrible,
It's short.
With snows in proper season,
Each burdens down the larch.
But March is full of treason,
And I hate March.

Hold your hats and duck, boys, March is nearly due,
The sleet is on the windowpane, the slush is on the shoe.
The pneumococcus carols a loud, triumphant song,
And not a holiday's in sight the whole month long.

On many a wedding present
In June my ducats fly.
The temperature's unpleasant
In July.
As August airs grow olden,
Hay fever's what I've got.
But any time seems golden
Compared to you-know-what.

Pick your shovels up, lads, you'll never know reprieve,
For March is on the threshold with a blizzard up its sleeve,
With a pussy-willow fable that is feeble on its facts,
And a brand-new estimation of your extra income tax.

October leaves I rake with
An ardor far from faint,
And April wetting take with-
Out complaint.
Serene, in weather lawful,
I shiver or I parch.
But March is merely awful.
I can't stand March.

Away, that month despicable, those days of dread and doubt,
When the gale blows down the chimney and the oil is running out.
(Besides, I own a private cause to call the time accurst—
I'll have another birthday when it's March the twenty-first.)

The Seven Ages of a Newspaper Subscriber

From infancy, from childhood's earliest caper,
He loved the daily paper.

Propped on his grubby elbows, lying prone,
He took, at first, the Comics for his own.
Then, as he altered stature and his voice,
Sports were his single choice.

For a brief time, at twenty, Thought became
A desultory flame.
So with a critic eye he would peruse
The better Book Reviews.

Behold the bridegroom, then—the dazzled suitor
Turned grim commuter,
Learning without direction
To fold his paper to the Housing Section.

Forty enlarged his waistline with his wage.
The Business Page
Engrossed his mind. He liked to ponder well
The charted rise of Steel or Tel & Tel.

Choleric, pompous, and too often vext,
The fifties claimed him next.
The Editorials, then, were what he scanned.
(Even, at times, he took his pen in hand.)

But witness how the human viewpoint varies:
Of late he reads the day's Obituaries.

To a Lady in a Phone Booth

Plump occupant of Number Eight,
    Outside whose door I shift my parcels
And wait and wait and wait and wait
    With aching nerves and metatarsals,
I long to comprehend the truth:
What keeps you sitting in that booth?

What compact holds you like a stone?
    Whose voice, whose summons rich with power,
Has fixed you to the telephone
    These past three-quarters of an hour?
Can this be love? Or thorns and prickles?
And where do you get all those nickels?

Say, was the roof above you sold
    By nameless landlord, cruel and craven,
Till, driven by imperious cold,
    You find this nook your only haven?
Yield me the instrument you hoard,
And I will share my bed and board.

Perhaps you choose such public place
    To do your lips and change your vesture.
You have not swooned, in any case.
    A motion, an occasional gesture,
Assures me you are safe inside.
You do not sleep. You have not died.

That paper clutched within your fist—
    I cannot quite make out the heading—
Madam, is that a formal list?
    Do you, by chance, arrange a wedding?
Or—dreadful thought I dare not speak!—
Perhaps you rent here by the week.

Well, likely I shall never know.
    My arches fall, my patience ravels.
And with these bundles I must go,
    Frustrated, forth upon my travels.
Behind the unrevealing pane
The mystery and you remain.

Yet, as I totter out of line,
    A faint suspicion waxes stronger.
Oh, could it be your feet, like mine,
    Would simply bear you up no longer?
So did you happen, unaware,
Upon this cubicle, with chair,

And did it seem in all the town
One spot where you could just sit down?

Subversive Reflections

If wit engendered worthy deed
    And only the good were gay,
Bad company would seldom lead
    The innocent astray.
Toward primrose pastures few would stir
    In search of light and color
Were virtuous people merrier
    Or the naughty people duller.

Old Gardener's Warning

Between one April's jonquil buds
   And the next spring's narcissus flowers,
There used to roll imperial floods
   Of months and weeks and days and hours.

The year went slow, the year went slow.
   It idled, almost to provoke us,
From the first flying of the snow
   Until the flaunting of the crocus,

And there was time to cope with roots
   Of irises, and be their master,
Or count the roses' earliest shoots
   Before one blinked and saw the aster.

But how a garden hurries now!
   The seasons blur and run together,
Leaf scarcely anchored to the bough
   Before October cuts its tether.

No vine may pause, no blossom stay
   For our regard. While lilacs hurtle,
Heedless and headlong, into May,
   The zinnia tramples down the myrtle.

And daffodils, before our eyes,
   Are caught beneath November's sickle
As the year shrinks to the day's size
   And the great flood becomes a trickle.

Quick! Run! Forbear to dillydally.
   Glance at the sky but do not mind it.
If here's the lily of the valley,
   Can winter now be far behind it?

Without Reservation

FRAGMENTS FROM THE DIARY OF A SUMMER TOURIST
IN CANADA

MOUNTAIN INTERLUDE

They might just as well
  Have been holding conventions
At every hotel
  In the Scenic Laurentians.

O GOD, O MONTREAL!

In Montreal, in Montreal,
  We saw two nuns with look seraphic.
We saw the rain incessant fall
  On us and on the tangled traffic.
We saw some interesting tombs,
  A park, full many a Gothic steeple,
An inn that boasts a thousand rooms
  (All saved for other people).

PASTORAL

At quaint, old-worldly Ste. Agathe,
We got a Room. But not a Bath.

MURRAY BAY

They had no vacancies for two
At Château Murray or the Richelieu.
So we did not stay
At Murray Bay.

ANCIENT CITY

Streets of Quebec are charming to remember—
  Steep, cobbled, wearing courtyards at the back,
Called by the names of saints. (Booked till September
  We found the Frontenac.)
Along the river, youth went promenading
  That summer eve. We watched them from a bench,

Then ate a dinner à la carte, applauding
   Each other's French.
The Clarendon regretted. We fell heir to
   Some guesthouse chamber, showerless and hot.
At morning we departed, taking care to
   Garder la droite.

To a Talkative Hairdresser

Too garrulous minion, stop. Be dumb.
   Attend my curls, however tarnished,
In silence. Sir, I did not come
   For your opinion, plain or varnished.

I do not wish to hear your views.
   The time is ripe for no discussion
Of hemlines current in the news,
   Politics, weather, or the Russian.

Spare me the story (while you soap)
   Of how your molars lately acted.
This little hour—or so I hope—
   Is mine for languor undistracted.

Calm is this air-conditioned grot.
   I drowse, and there might linger in me
An unaccustomed peace, but not
   If you must babble as you pin me,

If you must feel impelled to break
   My slumber with your conversation
Concerning modes, the price of steak,
   Or where you went on your vacation.

Hush! Fetch me *Vogue* and get me to
   The dryer quickly as you can, sir,
Which drones no windier than you
   Or duller, nor expects an answer.

Ballad of Blue-Plate Specials

Gone are the days when myself was young and lissom,
  Gone like nickel candy bars and kings and 'possum coats.
The snows of yesteryear are gone and few there are that miss 'm.
  But I lament the Dollar Table d'Hôtes.

> Do you mind the Dollar Dinner?
>   Do you recollect the fare
> That was proffered saint or sinner
>   Once at tables everywhere?
> Not a tearoom in the city,
>   Scarce a tavern in the town
> But would serve you something pretty
>   If you laid a dollar down.

I remember, I remember, how the candles used to gutter,
  How the napkins made of paper from one's lap were wont to slip.
Oh, the spoonbread with the chicken! Oh, the flower-printed butter!
  Oh, the curtsy when you left a quarter tip!

> On the daily Dollar Dinner,
>   There was choice of pot. or veg.,
> There was soup as a beginner,
>   There was pie with fluted edge.
> In its season corn was cob-ish,
>   And the relishes were tart.
> Only captious folk or snobbish
>   Ever ordered à la carte.

You may seek the ancient restaurants but little will it gain you,
  Though Musak plays as sweetly and the hostess smiles as pert.
For in lone, expensive glory stands the entree on the menu,
  And tomato juice is extra like dessert.

> Though the bouillon's just as pallid,
>   And as dubious the glass,

Now it's extra for the salad.
  Extra comes the demitasse.
And the cream, it runneth thinner
Than it did in days of yore
Since the darling Dollar Dinner,
The delicious Dollar Dinner,
The beparsleyed Dollar Dinner
  Stars the bill of fare no more.
(I just ate a dollar dinner
  But it cost me nearly four.)

Poem in Praise of the Continental Congress

A FOURTH OF JULY HYMN

Thank you, Mr. Jefferson,
  For bearding the British brass.
And thank you, Mr. Adams,
  Of Braintree (Quincy), Mass.
Carroll and Clark and Clymer,
  Harrison, Hancock, Hart,
Printer Franklin and Planter Hall,
I thank you one and I thank you all
For rising up at your country's call
  And giving the Fourth a start.
Thanks with gratitude more than cursory
For handing July an anniversary.

What is so rare in these sovereign states
As festive weather on festive dates?
Sneezes hamper the Yuletide kiss.
Autumn glooms on the Armistice.
Easter's certain to be contrary.
Washington picked out February.
But east and west and south and north
There's strawberry shortcake on the Fourth.

So hip and hip and a loud hooray
For glorious Independence Day,
Day auspicious for every comer
Because it falls on the Fourth of summer,
When winds are soft and the air's a prism
And climate's conducive to patriotism.
Fathers, I'm grateful when I remember
You might have fixed on the Fourth of November.

You might have chosen August,
   When lawns begin to parch,
Defended Man in the middle of Jan.
   Or the horrible first of March.
But you thought of parades and picnics,
   Of a blue American sky,
Of driving fast in a brand-new car,
Of rowing boats and of breaking par,
And you set it down on your calendar
   That you'd choose the Fourth of July.

So thank you, Button Gwinnett,
   For a celebration blithe.
And thank you, Roger Sherman,
   And thank you, Mr. Wythe.
Hopkinson, Hooper, Heyward,
   Livingston, Lewis, Lee,
Merchant Morris, of Morrisania,
Morton, the jurist from Pennsylvania,
I'm happy you surged with that freedomania.
   Thanks for the Land of the Free,
For giving us liberty's deathless chime
And a holiday in the summertime.

Notes on Literary Revivals

It's hard
Keeping up with the *avant-garde*.
There was the time that Donne
Had a place in the sun.
His *lettres* were *belles* of pure gold
And they tolled and they tolled and they tolled,
Until critics in suitable haunts
Took up Kafka (Franz).
Then everyone wanted to herald
The genius of Scott Fitzgerald.
After that, among Prominent Names,
It was utterly Henry James.

In between, of course, there was room
For a Melville boom,
For a peek at Poe, for a dollop
Of Trollope,
And currently people report on
A scrambling aboard
The elegant wagons of Wharton
And Ford Madox Ford.

Oh, it's perfectly clear
That there's change when the critics forgather.
Last year was a Hawthorne year.
Coming up—Willa Cather?

And I'm happy the great ones are thriving,
But what puzzles my head
Is the thought that they needed reviving.
I had never been told they were dead.

Literary Landscape with Dove and Poet

OR, VERSES IN THE MODERN MANNER

The pedant dove, the poet who admires him
Are adepts, both, of a most natural style.
Each is aware that music needs no meaning.

"Coo, coo," observes the dove all morning long,
All morning long, all evening longer still.
Mourning and evening are his occupations.

While underneath his eaves of occupation,
Dove-plump with melody, the poet murmurs
"Coo, coo," incessant as a chime of bills.

Each is aware that music needs no meaning
Since the instructed and submissive ear
Believes the Word: "Coo, coo" is metaphysics.

Complaint in Womrath's

My library lamp would burn more midnight watts
Could I come on a novel that wasn't about tots,
Could I open a book that didn't contain the essence
Of secret childhood or wistful adolescence,
Distilled (into four hundred pages, preface and all)
By an author afflicted with Style and Total Recall.

For the young, if they're kept out of sight, I've a deal of
        forbearance.
I realize modern babes must resent their parents,
Fall in love with their nursemaids, look on with innocent frown
While someone is murdered or playmates tactlessly drown,
And I comprehend that it's perfectly normal in kiddos
For little girls to be deadlier than Black Widows.

I understand all that. Still, I've never been wild
About viewing the world through the eyes of a sensitive child

Or even insensitive ones. Let me pulse, when I pulse,
Over gruesome adventures happening to adults.
The pangs that inferior Juliets feel as they grow up
Induce in me but a delicate yearning to throw up.

Ah, bring me a book
Where hero and heroine both wear that weathered look!

I'll settle for something historical, something post-Freudian,
Something purple or tough or suspenseful or plain celluloidian,
Something arty or artless, something even by Henry Green,
So long as it's peopled by characters over sixteen.

For the tale of a child may be teeming with local color,
But bores will be bores
And the younger they come, the duller.

Public Journal

*Verses inspired by a day spent in communion with the bright young
men of English verse*

It is four in the afternoon. Time still for a poem,
A poem not topical, wholly, or romantic, or metaphysic,
But fetched from the grab-bag of my mind and gaudy with
Symbol, slogan, quotation, and even music.
And many a Marxian maxim and many allusions
To a daft system and a world-disorder.
I will mention machines and the eight-hour day and
Czechoslovakia and the invaded border.

I will speak of love and I will do it slyly,
Unloosing the sacred girdle with a tired air,
Taking particular pains to notice the elastic garters
And the literal underwear.

I will put learning into my poem, for I acquired learning
At Cambridge or Oxford, it does not matter which.

But I'll freshen it up with slang which I got by ear,
Though it may sound a little off pitch.
And I'll be casual with rhymes for that is the trend,
Fashionable as the black hat of Anthony Eden.
I may put them at the middle of the stanza instead of the end,
For really amazing effect.
Or perhaps I'll find that assonance heightens the meaning better.
Yes, definitely, I prefer the latter.

Well, it will be sport, writing my private hates
And my personal credo.
I must bring in how I went to Spain on a holiday,
And how cold it was in Toledo.
There was a bootblack, too, in Madrid,
Who gave my shoes a burnish.
He told me something important which I cannot repeat,
For though I understand Spain, I do not understand Spanish.

I will put tarts into my poem, and tenement people,
The poor but not the meek;
And pieces of popular songs for a hint of nostalgia,
And bits of Greek.

I shall be tough and ardent and angry-eyed,
Aware that the world is dying, gasping, its face grown pallid;
But quick to embalm it in language as an aspic
Enfolds the chicken salad.

Now it is five o'clock. The poem is finished
Like Poland, like the upper classes, like Sunday's roast.
I must straighten my waistcoat and see that it goes straight out
By the evening post.

For what is left for us? Only
The stanza a day,
And the American royalties, and an inherited income,
To keep the wolf at bay.

Advice to a Young Person About to Write a Book with No Equipment Other than Talent

Anachronistic stripling,
    If you would see your name
In living letters rippling
    Across the scroll of fame,
Then shun those regions airy
    Where geniuses are made,
Lay down the dictionary,
    And learn another trade.
For not among the dwellers
    On bleak Parnassian heights
Are born the sleek best-sellers
    Complete with movie rights.

Fatuous boy, to art apprenticed,
Leave your Muse and be a dentist,
Be an actor, be a hoofer,
Welder, architect, or roofer.
Chart the heavens' starry courses,
Ride the rails or play the horses.
Have a hobby, keep a pet,
Photograph the Soviet.
Build a dam or paint a steeple,
Or just know a lot of people
And with anecdote and hint
Scandalize them well in print.
Then what radiance will flash off
From the volume that you dash off!

His royalties are slighter,
    And meager grow the bays
For any simple writer
    Who loves the polished phrase.
He gives his strict attention
    To Character and Style,

And lands in "Briefer Mention"
  And ends on Liggett's aisle.
But scrivening physicians
  Or raconteurs in pubs
Recount their twelve editions
  For Book-and-Author Clubs.

Therefore, stripling, if you choose
To acquire the best reviews,
Join the circus, buy a dairy,
Be an expert military,
Be a captain on a liner,
Lawyer, preacher, dress-designer,
Rich man, poor man, beggar, thief,
Someone lately on relief,
Dodger, weary of the bat,
Reminiscent diplomat.
But the best of all to be
Is some sort of refugee.
Then, with contracts tailored to you
How the publishers will woo you.

Art, lad, is an eccentricity,
But sweet are the uses of publicity.

Reflections on the Benefits of Keeping a Journal

LIVES of great men point a moral:
  We should prosper in our primes
And, retiring, wreathed with laurel,
  Sell our memoirs to the *Times*.

DOMESTIC AFFAIRS

About Children

By all the published facts in the case,
Children belong to the human race.

Equipped with consciousness, passions, pulse,
They even grow up and become adults.

So why's the resemblance, moral or mental,
Of children to people so coincidental?

Upright out of primordial dens,
Homo walked and was sapiens.

But rare as leviathans or auks
Is—male or female—the child who walks.

He runs, he gallops, he crawls, he pounces,
Flies, leaps, stands on his head, or bounces,

Imitates snakes or the tiger stripèd
But seldom recalls he is labeled "Biped."

Which man or woman have you set sights on
Who craves to slumber with all the lights on

Yet creeps away to a lampless nook
In order to pore on a comic book?

Why, if (according to A. Gesell)
The minds of children ring clear as a bell,

Does every question one asks a tot
Receive the similar answer—"What?"

And who ever started the baseless rumor
That any child has a sense of humor?

Children conceive of no jest that's madder
Than Daddy falling from a ten-foot ladder.

Their fancies sway like jetsam and flotsam;
One minute they're winsome, the next they're swatsome.

While sweet their visages, soft their arts are,
Cold as a mermaiden's kiss their hearts are;

They comprehend neither pity nor treason.
An hour to them is a three months' season.

So who can say—this is just between us—
That children and we are a common genus,

When the selfsame nimbus is eerily worn
By a nymph, a child, and a unicorn?

Young Man with an Heir

From what majestic portals,
    From what Olympian ways,
You fix on common mortals
    Your condescending gaze,
Who—entering the nursery
    And halting at the door—
Have in one moment cursory
    Become an Ancestor.

This infant, red and slumbering,
    That you've so lately met—
This morsel now encumbering
    Crib, scales, or bassinet—
In him I watch you test your
    Resemblance and your mark
And straightway don the vesture
    That robes a Patriarch.

Even as you were bending
    Above your scion, now,
I saw the crown descending
    To your astonished brow.
And on your shaven chin, sir,
    I noticed as I peered,
Indubitably began, sir,
    A faint, ancestral beard.

Before your startled stare looms
    What venerable reward!
Your chattels all turn heirlooms,
    Yourself a Foundling Lord.
And, seeing your look engravèd
    On one pink, new-born lamb,
You range yourself with David,
    Solomon, Abraham.

Comeuppance for a Progeny

*"A credit of $400 may be claimed for each person . . . under eighteen
years of age."*   —*Federal Income-Tax Report.*

Arrogant girl,
   Unclasp that curl
And stifle that forward dimple.
When I swore your worth
Was the wealth of earth,
   I find I was fond and simple.
I set your price, and I set it high,
   You personal bundle from heaven, you;
But look at the market as quoted by
   The Collector of Internal Revenue!

You, our costly, our first edition,
A mine of gold to the obstetrician,
To the corner druggist whose bills unnerve us,
To Kiddie Krackers and Diaper Servus;
You, our treasure, our platinum tot,
For whom we mortgaged the house and lot,
Had better develop a sense of humor.
You're worth four hundred and not a sou more.

Cherubic tumbler,
Be meek, be humbler,
   Of tempers and tantrums, wary.
Your infant charm
May possibly warm
   The heart of the Golden Dairy.
But hushaby, baby, cease those pranks
   That harry your mom and popper.
They've got you down on the Income blanks
   At scarcely your weight in copper.

You who jingle like ready money
To him that fathered the Snuggle Bunny;

You, the original Comstock Lode
For all purveyors to our abode:
For makers of socks
   And hoods and gaiters,
Alphabet blocks
   And perambulators,
Cots and creepers
   And nursery stands,
Arnold sleepers
   And Carter bands,
Dolls and mittens
And oilcloth kittens
And christening mugs
And cribs
And bibs—
You, who rate, when the books are done,
As Luxury Item Number One,
Are here recorded beyond redemption
As four hundred dollars tax exemption.

Collector's Items

Some lives are filled with sorrow and woe
   And some with joys ethereal.
But the days may come and the weeks may go,
   My life is filled with cereal.
My cupboards bulge and my shelves are bunchy
With morsels crispy or cracked or crunchy,
With rice things, corn things,
   Barley things, wheaten—
All top-of-the-morn things
   And all uneaten.
Ignored they sparkle, unheard they pop
When once they've yielded the Premium Top.

For Cheerios may be just the fare
   To energize whippersnappers,

But mine consider they've had their share
    As soon as they've filched the wrappers.
Breathes there a child with hopes so dim
That Kix are innocent Kix to him,
Not loot for filling
    His crowded coffers
With Big New Thrilling
    Premium Offers?
If such (as I fervently doubt) there be,
He is no kin to my progeny.

As a gardener lusts for a marigold,
    As a miser loves what he mises,
So dotes the heart of a nine-year-old
    On sending away for prizes.
The postman rings and the mail flies hence
With Premium Tops and fifteen cents.
The postman knocks and the gifts roll in:
Guaranteed cardboard, genuine tin,
Paper gadgets and gadgets plastic,
Things that work till you lose the elastic,
Things to molder in draws and pockets,
Magnets, parachutes, pistols, rockets,
Weapons good for a cop's assistant,
Whistles for dogs that are nonexistent,
Toys designed
    To make mothers tremble,
That fathers find
    They have to assemble,
Things Tom Mixish or Supermanish.
How gadgets come and the box tops vanish!
Then hippity-hop
To the grocer's shop
For a brand-new brand with a Premium Top.

Oh, some lives read like an open book
    And some like a legend hoary.
But life to me, wherever I look,
    Seems one long cereal story.

One Crowded Hour of Glorious Strife

I love my daughters with a love unfailing,
I love them healthy and I love them ailing.
I love them as sheep are loved by the shepherd,
With a fiery love like a lion or a leopard.
I love them gentle or inclined to mayhem—
But I love them warmest after eight-thirty a.m.

Oh, the peace like heaven
    That wraps me around,
Say, at eight-thirty-seven,
    When they're schoolroom-bound
With the last glove mated
    And the last scarf tied,
With the pigtail plaited,
    With the pincurl dried,
And the egg disparaged,
    And the porridge sneered at,
And last night's comics furtively peered at,
The coat apprehended
    On its ultimate hook,
And the cover mended
    On the history book!

How affection swells, how my heart leaps up
As I sip my coffee from a lonely cup!
For placid as the purling of woodland waters
Is a house divested of its morning daughters.
Sweeter than the song of the lark in the sky
Are my darlings' voices as they shriek good-by—

With the last shoe burnished
    And the last pen filled,
And the bus fare furnished
    And the radio stilled;
When I've signed the excuses
    And written the notes,

And poured fresh juices
  Down ritual throats,
And rummaged for umbrellas
  Lest the day grow damper,
And rescued homework from an upstairs hamper,
And stripped my wallet
  In the daily shakedown,
And tottered to my pallet
  For a nervous breakdown.

Oh, I love my daughters with a love that's reckless
As Cornelia's for the jewels in her fabled necklace.
But Cornelia, even, must have raised three cheers
At the front door closing on her school-bent dears.

Death at Suppertime

Between the dark and the daylight,
  When the night is beginning to lower,
Comes a pause in the day's occupation,
  That is known as the Children's Hour.

That endeth the skipping and skating,
  The giggles, the tantrums, and tears,
When, the innocent voices abating,
  Alert grow the innocent ears.

The little boys leap from the stairways,
  Girls lay down their dolls on the dot,
For promptly at five o'er the airways
  Comes violence geared to the tot.

Comes murder, comes arson, come G-men
  Pursuing unspeakable spies;
Come gangsters and tough-talking he-men
  With six-shooters strapped to their thighs;

Comes the corpse in the dust, comes the dictum
  "Ya' better start singin', ya' rat!"

While the torturer leers at his victim,
    The killer unleashes his gat.

With mayhem the twilight is reeling.
    Blood spatters, the tommy guns bark.
Hands reach for the sky or the ceiling
    As the dagger strikes home in the dark.

And lo! with what rapturous wonder
    The little ones hark to each tale
Of gambler shot down with his plunder
    Or outlaw abducting the mail.

Between the news and the tireless
    Commercials, while tempers turn sour,
Comes a season of horror by wireless,
    That is known as the Children's Hour.

Here Come the Clowns, Didn't They?

Oh, the tinted tanbark! Oh, the tangy airs!
Oh, the snobbish camels and the plump performing bears!
Oh, the plumèd horses! Oh, all I fail to see
When Dulcy's at the Circus,
Sitting next to me.

It's high wire and light wire
    And no net beneath;
The girl is on the tight wire.
    She wears a spangled sheath.
It's clasp hands and hope, now,
    Trembling below—
Dare she skip the rope, now?
    I'll never know.
For just as she's turning
    And drums have begun,
Dulcy gets a yearning
    For a frankfurter bun.

Yoo-hoo, wiener man! Hurry with your pitch.
Dulcy has an appetite, so spread the mustard rich.
Give the man the money, dear; bid the man begone.
Now let's watch the lady—
But the next act's on.

> The spot's glowing yellow,
> > Weak grow the knees,
> See the daring fellow
> > On aerial trapeze.
> The thunder of voices
> > Is hushed as by sleep.
> But just as he poises,
> > Tense, for the leap,
> Dimmed is the splendor,
> > For, heading our way,
> Dulcy spies the vendor
> > With the ice-cream tray.

Is the diver rescued, flashing as he falls?
Can the juggler balance those thirty spinning balls?
Do the ponies samba, the tigers know their trade?
Comes a Circus crisis,
I'm buying lemonade.

> I am keeping handy
> > Quarters to swap
> For pink cotton candy
> > And warm bottled pop,
> For souvenir turtles
> > Alive and unfed,
> While Superman hurtles,
> > Ignored, overhead.
> But someday, ah, someday,
> > With heart light as foam,
> I'll hie to the Circus
> > Like pilgrim to Rome.
> I'm going to the Circus
> > And I'll leave my daughter home.

Plea in a Children's Bookshop

Do you have a book for a literate girl
   Who's six years old tomorrow?
A book to be read when it's time for bed
   And hidden from those who borrow?
She leans to the magic of just-suppose,
   She's fond of a tale that's merry,
But she doesn't care how the story goes
   Or whether it's true or fairy,
And she doesn't mind how the pictures look.
   She'd blink at a price inflation,
So long as the book is a regular book
   Instead of an Animation.

Sir or Madam, I beg you hop up.
Find her a volume that doesn't pop up,
Fold, make comical noises, bend,
Waggle, or wiggle, or stand on end—
Something not so up-to-the-minute,
That isn't sold with a record in it
Or a chime that rings if your fingers strike it.
It may be Art, but she doesn't like it.

Her eyes would glisten if she might listen
   To Sinbad the Sailor's progress.
With sweet compliance she'd hear of giants,
   Or ogres, or maybe an ogress.
She'd like a dwarf of a proper size
   Or a stepmother cruel and clever.
But she doesn't want them to roll their eyes,
   Propelled by a paper lever.
Away with audible tigers, please,
   And sheep (you can comb their wool out).
The lady's learning her A.B.C.s
   And she isn't amused by a Pull-out.

Seller of narratives juvenile,
Scan your counter and search your aisle.
Surely somewhere amid the welter
A book immobile is taking shelter
Whose pictured dragon, whose painted wizard
Wasn't designed to be stroked or scissored,
Pasted, colored, or strung with beading.
Haven't you anything meant for *reading?*

The Velvet Hand

I call that parent rash and wild
Who'd reason with a six-year child,
Believing little twigs are bent
By calm, considered argument.

In bandying words with progeny,
There's no percentage I can see,
And people who, imprudent, do so,
Will wonder how their troubles grew so.

Now underneath this tranquil roof
Where sounder theories have their proof,
Our life is sweet, our infants happy.
In quietude dwell Mammy and Pappy.

We've sworn a stern, parental vow
That argument we won't allow.
Brooking no juvenile excess here,
We say a simple No or Yes, here,

And then, when childish wails begin
We don't debate.
We just give in.

Anniversary

In garden-colored boots he goes
    Ardent around perennial borders
To spray the pink, celestial rose
    Or give a weed its marching orders.

Draining at dawn his hasty cup,
    He takes a train to urban places;
By lamplight, cheerful, figures up
    The cost of camps and dental braces.

And warm upon my shoulders lays
    Impetuous at dinner table
The mantle of familiar praise
    That's better than a coat of sable.

Letter from a Country Inn

Dinner's at one. They ring an outside gong
    To summon cottagers from down the hill.
The blue, anonymous days are seasons long,
    And nights derisive with a whippoorwill.

We brag on postal cards about the blankets
    We sleep beneath, or praise the altitude.
The meadow wears its butterflies like trinkets,
    Gaudy and inexhaustibly renewed.

And all the hours are loud with children falling
    From habitable trees or in the lake,
Forever at the tops of voices calling
    The gossip that consumes them while they wake,

Pursuing goose or fleeing jealous gander,
    Fishing for minnow fabulous as whale,

Or scooping up the luckless salamander
   From violated pool to secret pail.

Here time swings idly as a toy balloon,
   Empty of struggle, almost of thought itself.
Yesterday's paper comes this afternoon
   And lies unopened on the mantel shelf,

And all is innocent and desultory
   As we'd forgotten that a world might seem.
Only at week's end does the tempo vary.
   Then dreaming women rouse themselves from dream,

Tie ribbons in their hair with rapt attention,
   Discard their knitting, put their novels down,
And half-delighted, half with apprehension,
   Await the train that carries up from town

Their stranger husbands, fetching even here
Reality's outrageous atmosphere.

Departure from Vermont

   Close the last cupboard, roll the rug,
      Sweep clean the hearth of ash and splinter,
   Batten the final window snug
      Against imagined shapes of winter.

   The station wagon at the door
      Already pants for homeways hilly.
   This is farewell. One summer more
      Has withered like the Turk's-cap lily.

   Now mist and pallor overtake
      The meadows where we liked to forage;
   No swimmer cleaves the metal lake;
      Sailless, the sailboat sulks in storage.

Already cold the morning airs.
   At night the bullfrog counsels danger.
And this familiar landscape wears
   The sudden aspect of a stranger.

There lies a menace in the north.
   The swallows from their eaves have stolen.
So fetch the bursting luggage forth—
   Since June, miraculously swollen.

Discarding hammock to the moth,
   The picnic place to brush and boulder,
Now drape the unaccustomed cloth
   Of town upon the sunburnt shoulder.

This is farewell. Quick, turn the key
   Upon the cricket's parting sentence
And, newly waked from languor, flee
   The season's husk without repentance.

Two Poems from a Private Room

I. DON'T SHAKE THE BOTTLE, SHAKE YOUR MOTHER-IN-LAW

When I was young and full of rhymes
   And all my days were salady,
Almost I could enjoy the times
   I caught some current malady.
Then, cheerful, knocked upon my door
   The jocular physician,
With tonics and with comfort for
   My innocent condition.
Then friends would fetch me flowers
   And nurses rub my back,
And I could talk for hours
   Concerning my attack.
But now, when vapors dog me,
   What solace do I find?

My cronies can't endure me.
The doctors scorn to cure me,
And, though I ail, assure me
It's all a state of mind.

It's psychosomatic, now, psychosomatic.
Whatever you suffer is psychosomatic.
Your liver's a-quiver? You're feeling infirm?
Dispose of the notion you harbor a germ.
Angina,
    Arthritis,
        Abdominal pain—
They're nothing but symptoms of marital strain.
They're nothing but proof that your love life is minus.
The ego is aching
Instead of the sinus.
So face up and brace up and stifle that sneeze.
It's psychosomatic. And ten dollars, please.

There was a time that I recall,
    If one grew pale or thinnish,
The pundits loved to lay it all
    On foods unvitaminish,
Or else, dogmatic, would maintain
    Infection somewhere acted.
And when they'd shorn the tonsils twain,
    They pulled the tooth impacted.
But now that orgies dental
    Have made a modish halt,
Your ills today are mental
    And likely all your fault.
Now specialists inform you,
    While knitting of their brows,
Your pain, though sharp and shooting,
Is caused, beyond disputing,
Because you hate commuting
    Or can't abide your spouse.

It's psychosomatic, now, psychosomatic.
You fell down the stairway? It's psychosomatic.

That sprain of the ankle while waxing the floors—
You did it on purpose to get out of chores.
Nephritis,
    Neuritis,
        A case of the ague?
You're just giving in to frustrations that plague you.
You long to be coddled, beloved, acclaimed,
So you caught the sniffles.
And aren't you ashamed!
And maybe they're right. But I sob through my wheezes,
"They've taken the fun out of having diseases."

II. MESSAGE FOUND IN A BOTTLE
Thrown from a Window at Harkness Pavilion

When next upon my narrow cot,
    A prey to symptoms horrid,
I lie awake for fever's sake
    Or hold my aching forehead,
Let doctors come and doctors go,
    They'll meet with no resistance.
I'll gulp the bitterest brew. But, oh,
    Let nurses keep their distance.

For the hearts of nurses are solid gold
But their heels are flat and their hands are cold,
And their voices lilt with a lilt that's falser
Than the smile of an exhibition waltzer.
Yes, nurses can cure you, nurses restore you,
But nurses are bound that they'll do things for you.
They make your bed up
    On flimsy excuses.
They prop your head up
    And bring you juices.
They run with eggnogs from hither and thither.
They fling out your flowers before they wither.
They fetch your breakfast at dawn's first crack.
They keep on pleading to rub your back.
With eau de Cologne they delight to slosh you.
And over and over they want to wash you.

The nurse-at-night you can't recall.
　　She's vaguer than a dream is;
But when she whispers down the hall
　　You think you're *in extremis*.
The day nurse owns a beaming face
　　Designed to cheer and hearten,
And speaks to you with studied grace
　　As to a kindergarten.

Oh, the deeds of nurses are noble and pure,
But they're always taking your temperature.
And, dewy morn till the light grows paler,
They guard you close as a Nazi jailer.
They pull your shades and they shut your doors.
They snub convivial visitors.
Your veriest frown
　　They take to heart
And scribble it down
　　On a stealthy chart.
When you reach for a smoke they're there to nab you.
With pills they dose you, with needles they jab you.
They order you porridge instead of kippers.
They steal your pencils and hide your slippers.
They eat the candy your friends bequeath,
And hourly urge you to brush your teeth.

　　The tribe of Florence Nightingale,
　　　　Ah, let me not disparage.
　　How deft their ways with luncheon trays,
　　　　How masterful their carriage!
　　But when the pallid look I wear
　　　　That marks the Liquid Diet,
　　I wish they'd go some otherwhere
　　　　And let me groan in quiet,
　　Abandoned to my germy nest,
　　Unnursed, unlaundered, unoppressed.

Blues for a Melodeon

A castor's loose on the buttoned chair—
    The one upholstered in shabby coral.
I never noticed, before, that tear
    In the dining-room paper.

When did the rocker cease to rock,
    The fringe sag down on the corner sofa?
All of a sudden the Meissen clock
    Has a cherub missing.

All of a sudden the plaster chips,
    The carpet frays by the morning windows;
Careless, a rod from the curtain slips,
    And the gilt is tarnished.

This is the house that I knew by heart.
    Everything here seemed sound, immortal.
When did this delicate ruin start?
    How did the moth come?

Naked by daylight, the paint is airing
    Its rags and tatters. There's dust on the mantel.
And who is that gray-haired stranger staring
    Out of my mirror?

A WREATH OF CHRISTMAS

Dear Madam: We Know You Will
Want to Contribute . . .

Christmas is coming,
The geese are getting fat.
Please to put a penny in an old man's hat.
If you haven't got a penny, a ha'penny will do.
If you haven't got a ha'penny, God help you!

Please to put a nickel,
    Please to put a dime.
How petitions trickle
    In at Christmas time!
Come and Save a Scholar.
    Bring the heathen hope.
Just enclose a dollar
    Within the envelope.
Send along a tenner,
    Anyhow a five,
And let the Friends of Poetry inaugurate their drive.

Share your weekly ration
    With miners up in Nome.
Give a small donation
    To build a Starlings' Home.
Please to send a shillin'
    For lawyers in the lurch.

Drop a pretty bill in
   The offering at church.
Remember all the orphans,
   Recall the boys at camps,
And decorate your letters with illuminated stamps.

The Common Colds Committee
   Implores you to assist.
They're canvassing the city,
   They've got you on their list.
Demonstrate your mettle
   For half a hundred causes.
Fill the yawning kettle
   Of the corner Santa Clauses.
Give for holy Charity
   Wherever she appears.
And don't forget the Firemen and the Southern Mountaineers.

Christmas is coming,
The mail is getting fat.
Please to put a penny in every proffered hat.
If you haven't got a penny, a ha'pence let it be.
If you haven't got a ha'pence left, you're just like me.

City Christmas

Now is the time when the great urban heart
   More warmly beats, exiling melancholy.
Turkey comes table d'hôte or à la carte.
   Our elevator wears a wreath of holly.

Mendicant Santa Clause in flannel robes
   At every counter contradicts his label,
Alms-asking. We've a tree with colored globes
   In our apartment foyer, on a table.

There is a promise—or a threat—of snow
   Noised by the press. We pull our collars tighter.
And twenty thousand doormen hourly grow
   Politer and politer and politer.

Office Party

This holy night in open forum
   Miss McIntosh, who handles Files,
Has lost one shoe and her decorum.
   Stately, the frozen chairman smiles

On Media, desperately vocal.
   Credit, though they have lost their hopes
Of edging toward an early Local,
   Finger their bonus envelopes.

The glassy boys, the bursting girls
   Of Copy, start a Conga clatter
To a swung carol. Limply curls
   The final sandwich on the platter

Till hark! a herald Messenger
   (Room 414) lifts loudly up
His quavering tenor. Salesmen stir
   Libation for his Lily cup.

"Noel," he pipes, "Noel, Noel."
   Some wag beats tempo with a ruler.
And the plump blonde from Personnel
   Is sick behind the water cooler.

What Every Woman Knows

When little boys are able
   To comprehend the flaws
In their December fable
   And part with Santa Claus,
Although I do not think they grieve,
How burningly they disbelieve!

They cannot wait, they cannot rest
For knowledge nibbling at the breast.
They cannot rest, they cannot wait
To set conniving parents straight.

Branding that comrade as a dunce
Who trusts the saint they trusted once,
With rude guffaw and facial spasm
They publish their iconoclasm,
And find particularly shocking
The thought of hanging up a stocking.

But little girls (no blinder
   When faced by mortal fact)
Are cleverer and kinder
   And brimming full of tact.
The knowingness of little girls
Is hidden underneath their curls.

Obligingly, since parents fancy
The season's tinsel necromancy,
They take some pains to make pretense
Of duped and eager innocence.

Agnostics born but Bernhardts bred,
They hang the stocking by the bed,
Make plans, and pleasure their begetters
By writing Santa lengthy letters,

Only too well aware the fruit
Is shinier plunder, richer loot.

For little boys are rancorous
When robbed of any myth,
And spiteful and cantankerous
To all their kin and kith.
But little girls can draw conclusions
And profit from their lost illusions.

Lady Selecting Her Christmas Cards

Fastidiously, with gloved and careful fingers,
    Through the marked samples she pursues her search.
Which shall it be: the snowscape's wintry languors
    Complete with church,

An urban skyline, children sweetly pretty
    Sledding downhill, the chaste, ubiquitous wreath,
Schooner or candle or the simple Scottie
    With verse underneath?

Perhaps it might be better to emblazon
    With words alone the stiff, punctilious square.
(Oh, not Victorian, certainly. This season
    One meets it everywhere.)

She has a duty proper to the weather—
    A Birth she must announce, a rumor to spread,
Wherefore the very spheres once sang together
    And a star shone overhead.

Here are the Tidings which the shepherds panted
    One to another, kneeling by their flocks.
And they will bear her name (engraved, not printed),
    Twelve-fifty for the box.

Christmas Eve in Our Village

Main Street is gay. Each lamppost glimmers,
   Crowned with a blue, electric star.
The gift tree by our fountain shimmers,
   Superbly tall, if angular
   (Donated by the Men's Bazaar).

With garlands proper to the times
   Our doors are wreathed, our lintels strewn.
From our two steeples sound the chimes,
   Incessant, through the afternoon,
   Only a little out of tune.

Breathless, with boxes hard to handle,
   The grocery drivers come and go.
Madam the Chairman lights a candle
   To introduce our club's tableau.
   The hopeful children pray for snow.

They cluster, mittened, in the park
   To talk of morning, half affrighted,
And early comes the winter dark
   And early are our windows lighted
   To beckon homeward the benighted.

The eggnog's lifted for libation,
   Silent at last the postman's ring,
But on the plaza near the station
   The carolers are caroling.
   "O Little Town!" the carolers sing.

Twelfth Night

Down from the window take the withered holly.
Feed the torn tissue to the literal blaze.
Now, now at last are come the melancholy
Anticlimactic days.

Here in the light of morning, hard, unvarnished,
Let us with haste dismantle the tired tree
Of ornaments, a trifle chipped and tarnished,
Pretend we do not see

How all the rooms seem shabbier and meaner
And the tired house a little less than snug.
Fold up the tinsel. Run the vacuum cleaner
Over the littered rug.

Nothing is left. The postman passes by, now,
Bearing no gifts, no kind or seasonal word.
The icebox yields no wing, no nibbled thigh, now,
From any holiday bird.

Sharp in the streets the north wind plagues its betters
While Christmas snow to gutters is consigned.
Nothing remains except the thank-you letters,
Most tedious to the mind,

And the gilt gadget (duplicated) which is
Marked for exchange at Abercrombie-Fitch's.

The Thirties

PERSONAL REMARKS

Lament for a Wavering Viewpoint

I want to be a Tory
    And with the Tories stand,
Elect and bound for glory
    With a proud, congenial band.
Or in the Leftist hallways
    I gladly would abide,
But from my youth I always
    Could see the Other Side.

How comfortable to rest with
    The safe and armored folk
Congenitally blessed with
    Opinions stout as oak.
Assured that every question
    One single answer hath,
They keep a good digestion
    And whistle in their bath.

But all my views are plastic,
    With neither form nor pride.
They stretch like new elastic
    Around the Other Side;
And I grow lean and haggard
    With searching out the taint

Of hero in the Blackguard
Of villain in the saint.

Ah, snug lie those that slumber
Beneath Conviction's roof.
Their floors are sturdy lumber,
Their windows, weatherproof.
But I sleep cold forever
And cold sleep all my kind,
Born nakedly to shiver
In the draft from an open mind.

Ode to the End of Summer

Summer, adieu.
                    Adieu, gregarious season.
Good-by, 'revoir, farewell.
Now day comes late; now chillier blows the breeze on
Forsaken beach and boarded-up hotel.
Now wild geese fly together in thin lines
And Tourist Homes take down their lettered signs.

It fades—this green, this lavish interval,
This time of flowers and fruits,
Of melon ripe along the orchard wall,
Of sun and sails and wrinkled linen suits;
Time when the world seems rather plus than minus
And pollen tickles the allergic sinus.

Now fugitives to farm and shore and highland
Cancel their brief escape.
The Ferris wheel is quiet at Coney Island
And quaintness trades no longer on the Cape;
While meek-eyed parents hasten down the ramps
To greet their offspring, terrible from camps.

Turn up the steam. The year is growing older.
The maple boughs are red.
Summer, farewell. Farewell the sunburnt shoulder,
Farewell the peasant kerchief on the head.
Farewell the thunderstorm, complete with lightning,
And the white shoe that ever needeth whitening.

Farewell, vacation friendships, sweet but tenuous.
Ditto to slacks and shorts.
Farewell, O strange compulsion to be strenuous
Which sends us forth to death on tennis courts.
Farewell, Mosquito, horror of our nights;
Clambakes, iced tea, and transatlantic flights.

Unstintingly I yield myself to Autumn
And Equinoctial sloth.
I hide my swim suit in the bureau's bottom
Nor fear the fury of the after-moth.
Forswearing porch and pool and beetled garden,
My heart shall rest, my arteries shall harden.

Welcome, kind Fall, and every month with "r" in
Whereto my mind is bent.
Come, sedentary season that I star in,
O fire-lit Winter of my deep content!
Amid the snow, the sleet, the blizzard's raw gust,
I shall be cozier than I was in August.

Safe from the picnic sleeps the unlittered dell.
The last Good Humor sounds its final bell,
And all is silence.
                                        Summer, farewell, farewell.

Letter from a Winter Resort

The breeze is soft, the sky is blue,
   The sun's a gold persimmon;
But how dismaying to the view,
   This wilderness of women!
Upon the porches, ladies knit
   With small, well-practiced motion,
And ladies on the beaches sit,
   And ladies fill the ocean.

Brown-limbed, the little children play,
   Beside the rolling waters,
Or loudly dabble in the spray—
   And all of them are daughters.
Soprano voices cleave the air
   Or mingle in the houses.
It's women, women everywhere
   Except for furtive spouses.

Oh, tell me—for I half forget—
Are somewhere men surviving yet?
Not myth or tale or ancient fable,
Still do they lean across the table
In clubs and grills and automats,
And practice law and furnish flats
And work and play and take up hobbies
And meet you in predestined lobbies
And boast about their season's sales
And criticize your fingernails
And telephone from Frank-and-Gus's
And jostle you on "L"s and buses
And stand at bars with other hearties
And bring you drinks at cocktail parties
And tip their hats and swing their sticks
And argue over politics?
Oh, is it true, I ask again,
The world's still full of single men,

Ubiquitous as Cellophane,
    As commonplace as slumber,
Who hail you taxis in the rain
    And ask you for your number?
For what avails this winter rose,
    This January greenery,
Where nothing in profusion grows
    Save womankind and scenery?

This sky is blue, this air is sweet
    And soothing to the spirit,
But any Eden's incomplete
    With Adam nowhere near it.
Give me, instead, the frozen town
    And some alert defender.
For Holiday's no proper noun
    When feminine's the gender.

Notes for a Southern Road Map

Carry me back to old Virginny,
    Land of cotton and the Williamsburg Plan,
Where the banjo calls to the pickaninny
    And the sun never sets on the Ku Klux Klan.
Carry me anywhere south of the line, there,
    To old Kentucky or Fla. or Tenn.,
But when I hear that it's time to dine, there,
    You can carry me North again.
For Dixie's myth is a myth I dote on;
    The South's my mammy is what I mean.
But never, ah never, they'll get my vote on
    Their pet cuisine.

For it's ham,
Ham,
Frizzled or fried,
Baked or toasted,

Or on the side.
Ham for breakfast
And ham for luncheon,
Nothing but ham to sup or munch on.
Ham for dinner and ham for tea,
Ham from Atlanta
To the sea,
With world-worn chicken for change of venue,
But ham immutable on the menu.

Dear to my heart are the Southland's bounties,
    Where honeysuckle is sweet in May,
Where warble the Byrds from important counties
    And everything runs by the TVA.
I love the mint that they spice the cup with,
    Their women fair and their horses fast;
An accent, even, can I put up with,
    And stories, suh, from a Noble Past.
So carry me back to an old plantation
    In North Carolina or Alabam',
But succor me still from a steadfast ration
    Of ham.

Ham,
Ham,
Not lamb or bacon
But ham in Raleigh
And ham in Macon.
Ham for plutocrats,
Ham for pore folk,
Ham in Paducah and ham in Norfolk;
In Memphis, ham, and in Chapel Hill,
Chattanooga,
And Charlottesville.
Ham for the Missy,
Ham for the Colonel,
And for the traveler, Ham Eternal.

Oh, patriotically I implore,
Look away, Dixieland, from the smokehouse door.

The Purist

He sauntered through the pearly town,
  Critical, chill, aloof,
And favored Heaven with a frown
  Of casual reproof;

Observed the scrolls upon the gate,
  The moons, the rings-of-Saturn,
And doubted that they followed straight
  The ancient classic pattern,

Then tasted the eternal bread
  And sipped the unfailing wine.
"A vintage only fair," he said,
  "Scarce the authentic Vine."

He strolled to Time's extremest rim
  And stopped, and cupped his ears,
And presently there came to him
  The music of the spheres.

He sighed, "They flatted once or twice,
  Though pleasant enough they played."
So, for a while, through Paradise
  Mirth drooped and was dismayed,

Till suddenly a little gust
  (Breath of his own disdain)
Blew up and scattered him like dust
  Along the starry plain.

Lament of the Normal Child

The school where I go is a modern school
  With numerous modern graces.
And there they cling to the modern rule
  Of "Cherish the Problem Cases!"
From nine to three
I develop Me.
  I dance when I'm feeling dancy,
Or everywhere lay on
With creaking crayon
  The colors that suit my fancy.
But when the commoner tasks are done,
  Deserted, ignored, I stand.
For the rest have complexes, everyone;
  Or a hyperactive gland.
Oh, how can I ever be reconciled
  To my hatefully normal station?
Why couldn't I be a Problem Child
  Endowed with a small fixation?
Why wasn't I trained for a Problem Child
  With an Interesting Fixation?

I dread the sound of the morning bell.
  The iron has entered my soul.
I'm a square little peg who fits too well
  In a square little normal hole.
For seven years
In Mortimer Sears
  Has the Oedipus angle flourished;
And Jessamine Gray,
She cheats at play
  Because she is undernourished.
The teachers beam on Frederick Knipe
  With scientific gratitude,
For Fred, they claim, is a perfect type
  Of the Antisocial Attitude.

And Cuthbert Jones has his temper riled
   In a way professors mention.
But I am a Perfectly Normal Child,
   So I don't get any attention.
I'm nothing at all but a Normal Child,
   So I don't get the least attention.

The others jeer as they pass my way.
   They titter without forbearance.
"He's Perfectly Normal," they shrilly say,
   "With Perfectly Normal parents."
I learn to read
With a normal speed.
   I answer when I'm commanded.
Infected antrums
Don't give me tantrums.
   I don't even write left-handed.
I build with blocks when they give me blocks.
   When it's busy hour, I labor.
And I seldom delight in landing socks
   On the ear of my little neighbor.

So here, by luckier lads reviled,
   I sit on the steps alone.
Why couldn't I be a Problem Child
   With a Case to call my own?
Why wasn't I born a Problem Child
   With a Complex of my own?

Reflections Outside a Gymnasium

The belles of the eighties were soft,
 They were ribboned and ruffled and gored,
With bustles built proudly aloft
 And bosoms worn dashingly for'rd.
So, doting on bosoms and bustles,
 By fashion and circumstance pent,
They languished, neglecting their muscles,
 Growing flabby and plump and content,
Their most strenuous sport
 A game of croquet
On a neat little court
 In the cool of the day,
Or dipping with ladylike motions,
Fully clothed, into decorous oceans.

The eighties surveyed with alarm
 A figure long-legged and thinnish;
And they had not discovered the charm
 Of a solid-mahogany finish.
Of suns that could darken or speckle
 Their delicate skins they were wary.
They found it distasteful to freckle
 Or brown like a nut or a berry.
So they sat in the shade
 Or they put on a hat
And frequently stayed
 Fairly healthy at that
(And never lay nightlong awake
For sunburn and loveliness' sake).

When ladies rode forth, it was news,
 Though sidewise ensconced on the saddle.
And when they embarked in canoes
 A gentleman wielded the paddle.
They never felt urged to compete
 With persons excessively agile.

Their slippers were small on their feet
  And they thought it no shame to be fragile.
Could they swim? They could not.
  Did they dive? They forbore it.
And nobody thought
  The less of them for it.

No, none pointed out how their course was absurd,
Though their tennis was feeble, their golf but a word.
When breezes were chilly, they wrapped up in flannels,
They couldn't turn cartwheels, they didn't swim channels,
They seldom climbed mountains, and, what was more shocking,
Historians doubt that they even went walking.
If unenergetic,
  A demoiselle dared to
Be no more athletic
  Than ever she cared to.
Oh, strenuous comrades and maties,
How pleasant was life in the eighties!

Nursery Rhyme

Heigh ho,
This much I know:
What they say about men
Is largely so;
What they've told about women
From Eve to Ruth
Is sober counsel,
Is gospel truth;
Tabby and Thomas
Make dubious friends.
And that's where Wisdom
Begins and ends.

Ode to the Bath

"Dear to us ever is the banquet, and the harp, and the dance, and changes of raiment, and the warm bath, and love, and sleep."
—*From* The Odyssey, *Book VIII.*

Seven our sins are, and our virtues seven.
    Seven times ten our years' unwithered span.
And seven are the immortal mercies given
    To ease the lot of Man:
Slumber and food to keep his body whole,
    Fine raiment that proclaims his outward merit,
Motion, and music where he feeds his soul,
    And love to nurse his spirit—
These six are needful; but the seventh thing
    More constant succor hath.
Attend me, Muse, while loyally I sing
    The ancient consolation of the Bath.

      Yes, haste, Pieridian daughters;
        Assist me while I praise
      Those warm and living waters
        That comfort all my days.
      Shunning the upstart shower,
        The cold and cursory scrub,
      I celebrate the power
        That lies within the Tub.

For this alone of our enchantments seems
    Blessing without a barb.
The sleeper lies entangled in his dreams,
    The banquet ends in sodium bicarb.
The moth invades the coat, the harpers fail,
    The dance grows dull or all the dancers bedfast,
And love itself turns weary, flat, and stale.
    Only the Bath is steadfast,
Whose last caress is as the first embrace,
    Where limbs repose, the burdened shoulders sink,

And the lean mind, for half an hour's space,
Forbears to think.

    Not for the casual washer
      On simple cleanness bent,
    Not for the hasty splasher
      Awaits the Sacrament.
    Rewards are made to measure.
      And devotees recall
    That he who bathes for pleasure
      Must keep the ritual.

When spendthrift hand lay out the towels in order,
    Easy of access, fresh and soft as hope;
Let sponge be fluffy, but the brushes harder,
    And lathersome the soap.
Bring out the bath salts, decorously scented
    Of lavender or pine.
Bring pillow that the head may rest contented—
    Then turn the tap, release the flood divine
Till it three-quarters fill the porcelain chalice,
    Not cold or hot but tempered to desire.
And there's your refuge that was mankind's solace
    When Homer struck his lyre.

    For brighter joys may alter
      And livelier pastimes close,
    But in this happy shelter
      Peace blossoms like a rose.
    Of all refreshments primate,
      The last Beatitude,
    It keeps unchanging climate
      Where care may not intrude.
    Let others, worn with living
      And living's aftermath,
    Take Sleep to heal the heart's distress,
    Take Love to be their comfortress,
    Take Song or Food or Fancy Dress,
      But I shall take a Bath.

Dissertation on Furniture

Furniture's rather a good idea,
    And one that was early hit on.
Bureaus I'll pin to for stuffing things into,
    And sofas are nice to sit on.
Love seats cater to amorous souls,
    A mirror's a space-enhancer,
And secretaries have pigeonholes
    For letters you ought to answer.

But I sing the bed, oh, lovely device,
Flower of Furniture, Pearl without Price!
    Wide may its praises be spread.
For rugs they expect you to walk about on,
And desks were invented to work, no doubt, on,
But beds are things you can just stretch out on.
    I sing the bed!

A stove's the delight of an epicure
    Determined that he should sup right;
Pianos are grand for the strenuous band
    Who favor a posture upright;
A table's designed for holding lamps,
    And frequently, too, to eat off;
And fireplaces scatter the dews and damps
    When janitors turn the heat off.

But I sing the bed, more precious than these,
Excellent vessel of comfort and ease
    And rest that is better than bread—
Dear to the heart when the night is lowering,
Dear before dinner when tempers are souring,
Dearest of all when the morn is flowering.
    I sing the bed!

Then here's to the pallet the poor man seeks,
    And here's to the couch of the wealthy,
A kindly spot when the brow is hot
    And kindlier, still, when healthy.
And here's to the article glorified
    By Messrs. De Mille and Simmons,
Where all men's ultimate joys abide,
    And probably, also, women's.

For a shelf with a book has a cultured look
    And spaces for vases to go on,
And a rocking chair is beyond compare
    For stubbing the midnight toe on.
But it's pleasant to write a letter in bed
And breakfast always tastes better in bed
And life seems almost inviting in bed
And books are more exciting in bed
And poems are often inspired in bed
And you hardly ever get tired in bed.

So I sing the bed, by day and by night
Luxury's pinnacle, final delight.
    Shelter for spirit and head,
For being born and, of course, for dying in,
For reading and writing and multiplying in,
For nodding and napping and just for lying in,
    I sing the bed.

Inventors, Keep Away from My Door

Ah, where's the patented device
That I can learn to master?
My icebox yields me melted ice,
My oven, but disaster.
From stranded cars it is my fate
To view the rural scenery;
For I'm the poor unfortunate
Undone by all machinery.

Other people's robots keep a willing head up.
All their cheerful keyholes welcome in the key.
Other people's toasters do not burn their bread up.
But nothing ever works for me.

The gadgets come, the gadgets go,
Ambitious for the attic.
Tune up my stubborn radio—
It screams with rage and static.
The vacuum sweeper roundabout
With slippery strength encoils me.
Locks treacherously lock me out.
The simple corkscrew foils me.

Other people's mousetraps sometimes bring a mouse down.
Other people's furnaces sing in cozy glee.
Mine huffs and it puffs till it brings the quaking house down.
Nothing ever runs for me.

The humblest tools in my abode
Know half a hundred ruses
To leak or sputter or explode,
Catch fire or short their fuses.
In all things made of steel or wire,
Inanimate, unholy,

There lurks some dark, ancestral ire
    Directed at me, solely;
There lurks some black, malicious spite
    Amid the wheels and prisms,
And what shall save me from the might
    Of wrathful mechanisms?

Other people's watches do not send them late for
    Amorous appointment or literary tea.
Other people's telephones bring the word they wait for.
    But *nothing* ever works for me.

Melancholy Reflections After a Lost Argument

I always pay the verbal score
    With wit, concise, selective.
I have an apt and ample store
    Of ladylike invective.

My mots, retorts, and quips of speech,
    Hilarious or solemn,
Placed end to end, no doubt, would reach
    To any gossip column.

But what avails the epigram,
    The clever and the clear shot,
Invented chiefly when I am
    The only one in earshot?

And where's the good of repartee
    To quell a hostile laughter,
That tardily occurs to me
    A half an hour after?

God rest you merry, gentlemen,
    Who nastily have caught
The art of always striking when
    The irony is hot.

Poor Timing

I sing Saint Valentine, his day,
  I spread abroad his rumor—
A gentleman, it's safe to say,
  Who owned a sense of humor.
Most practical of jokers, he,
  Who bade sweethearts make merry
With flowers and birds and amorous words,
  In the month of February.
The antic, frantic,
Unromantic
  Middle of February.

Now, April weather's fine and fair
  For love to get a start in.
And May abets a willing pair,
  And June you lose your heart in.
There's many a month when wooing seems
  Both suitable and proper.
But the mating call unseasonal
  Is bound to come a cropper.

When blizzards rage with might and main
  And a man's best friend's his muffler,
Pity the February swain,
  That sentimental snuffler,
Whose soul must surge, whose pulse must throb
  With passionate cadenza,
When he yearns instead for a cozy bed
  Alone with influenza.

When winds blow up and snow comes down
  And the whole gray world seems horrider,
And every lass that sulks in town
  Thinks wistfully of Florider,
Pity the chapped and wintry maid
  Who'd trade the arms that clasp her in,

For Vitamin A and a nasal spray
    And maybe a bottle of aspirin.

Who wants to bill, who cares to coo,
    Who longs for cherry-chopping,
When noses are red and fingers blue
    And the hemoglobin's dropping?
Let summer lovers droop and pine,
    Let springtime hearts be airy.
I wouldn't be anyone's Valentine
    In the month of February.
The spare-able, terrible,
Quite unbearable
    Middle of February.

Why, Some of My Best Friends Are Women

I learned in my credulous youth
    That women are shallow as fountains.
Women make lies out of truth
    And out of a molehill their mountains.
Women are giddy and vain,
    Cold-hearted or tiresomely tender;
Yet, nevertheless, I maintain
    I dote on the feminine gender.

For the female of the species may be deadlier than the male
But she can make herself a cup of coffee without reducing
The entire kitchen to a shambles.

Perverse though their taste in cravats
    Is deemed by their lords and their betters,
They know the importance of hats
    And they write you the news in their letters.
Their minds may be lighter than foam,
    Or altered in haste and in hurry,
But they seldom bring company home
    When you're warming up yesterday's curry.

And when lovely woman stoops to folly,
She does not invariably come in at four A.M.
Singing "Sweet Adeline."

Oh, women are frail and they weep.
　　They are recklessly given to scions.
But, wakened unduly from sleep,
　　They are milder than tigers or lions.
Women hang clothes on their pegs
　　Nor groan at the toil and the trouble.
Women have rather nice legs
　　And chins that are guiltless of stubble.
Women are restless, uneasy to handle,
But when they are burning both ends of the scandal,
They do not insist with a vow that is votive,
How high are their minds and how noble the motive.

As shopping companions they're heroes and saints;
They meet you in tearooms nor murmur complaints;
They listen, entranced, to a list of your vapors;
At breakfast they sometimes emerge from the papers;
A Brave Little Widow's not apt to sob-story 'em,
And they keep a cool head in a grocery emporium.
Yes, I rise to defend
　　The quite possible She.
For the feminine gend-
　　Er is O.K. by me.

Besides, everybody admits it's a Man's World.
And just look what they've done to it!

Complaint to the American Medical Association

*Concerning their members' unfair monopoly of best-selling
autobiographies and other fiction*

Of all God's creatures here below
    Whose feats confound the skeptic
I most admire the Medico,
    That hero antiseptic.
He has my heart, he has my hand,
    He has my utmost loyalties.
(He also has my tonsils and
    A lien on my royalties.)
For from the time he doth begin
His sacred tryst with medicine,
How noble, he! How never-tiring!
Not rain, nor heat, nor maids admiring,
Nor bills unpaid, nor farmers' hounds
Can stay him from his sleepless rounds.
More fleet than winners of the Bendix,
He hastens to the burst appendix,
Or breasts the blizzard cold and shivery
To make some rural free delivery.

Or if to ampler orbits whirled
    (As fate will sometimes toss us),
How he bestrides this narrow world,
    A medical Colossus!
Perhaps, his kit upon his back,
    He dares the jungle thickets,
Intent upon the fevered track
    Of yaws or mumps or rickets.

The chum of kings, the friend of presidents,
He makes the earth his private residence;
One day prescribing pills and pickups
To cure an emperor of hiccups,
The next in stricken cities stranded,
Combating scourges single-handed,

At peril of life, at risk of limb.
Yet do such deeds suffice for him?
No, no. In secret all the while
He's sought a Literary Style.

The pen (so springs the constant hope
    Of all devout physicians)
Is mightier than the stethoscope
    And runs to more editions.
So while he's waged bacillic wars,
    Or sewed a clever suture,
His mind has hummed with metaphors
    Laid up against the future.
Amid the knives and sterile gauzes
He's dreamt of modifying clauses,
And never gone to bed so late
His diary wasn't up to date,
As if he'd sworn an oath to follow
Both Harper Brothers and Apollo.
Oh, more than Einstein, more than Edison
I do admire the man of Medison.
He has my hand, he has my note,
He has those X-rays of my throat,
But is it fair he should lay claim to
The overcrowded writing game, too?

I eye askance those dubious laurels.
Where are his ethics? Where his morals?
In what brave school did he matriculate
That he should be so damned articulate?
And where's the seal to show his betters
He's certified a Man of Letters?

Professional sirs, I gravely doubt,
    In any really nice sense,
Your boys should practice thus without
    Their literary license.

Advice to a Tot About to Learn the Alphabet

Consider, child, be prudent.
 Rash infant, not so fast!
Oh, stay, my dimpled student,
 Unlettered to the last.
Unless you leap before you look,
 Your fate will be a trite one.
For first you'll learn to read a book
 And then you'll want to write one.
The Pulitzers, the Guggenheims,
 Will rank you with the winners.
You'll print a play, compose some rhymes,
And be reviewed in the Sunday *Times*
And get invited for your crimes
 To Literary Dinners.

You'll be a Guest of Honor on a small, gold chair,
Consuming filet mignon with a literary air.
You'll grace the Speakers' Table, with authors flanked about,
For the Culture Groups will get you if you don't watch out.

Between the lions and parrots,
 Behind the potted shrubs,
You'll munch on peas and carrots
 And talk to Women's Clubs.
'Mid microphones and ferny fronds
 You'll raise your cultured voice
So dowagers in diamonds
 Can listen and rejoice,
So folk who take their authors neat
 Can boast they lingered nigh one,
And from a paid, impartial seat
Can gaze upon you while you eat
And twitter that your book was *sweet,*
 But never, never buy one.

Oh, princes thrive on caviar, the poor on whey and curds,
And politicians, I infer, must eat their windy words.
It's crusts that feed the virtuous, it's cake that comforts sinners,
But writers live on bread and praise at Literary Dinners.

So shun this vain utensil
  Before it is too late.
Throw down the bitten pencil,
  Discard the perilous slate,
Else soon you'll start to scribble verse
  And then you'll write a tome,
And so you'll go from bad to worse
  And never dine at home.
You'll buy yourself an opera hat
  And learn to speak with unction
And end a Guest of Honor at
  A Literary Function.

You'll be a Guest of Honor on a hard, gold chair,
With your name upon the menu just below the bill of fare,
And you'll sing for your supper while the lesser authors pout,
For the Culture Clubs will get you if you don't watch out.

The Outcast

"Solitary reading wrong, says Adler. . . . Likens it to drinking alone."
—*Headlines in the* New York Times.

Consider the poor sinner,
The desperate wretch by decency forsook,
Who, after dinner,
Stealthily from his shelves takes down a book
And like as not,
A drunken fool, a literary sot,
Creeps to his lonely cot,
There to swig down and out of public view
Immoderate tankards of the Pierian brew.

How sunk in vice is he! Look how he gloats,
Taking no notes,
Letting his febrile fancy roam at large in
Frivolous tomes and gay,
Despised by Mr. A.,
And annotating not a single margin.

Pity the fate
Of this inebriate.
Shunned by his fellows, none in his ear will shout
How the plot ended, how it all came out.
None in a Poetry Morning will enroll him,
No one will buttonhole him
To be an audience for some deathless prose
Recited through the nose.

But, all the precepts dead to,
Unsung at and unread to,
He'll end in squalor,
A miserable bookworm or a scholar.

Women of Jericho

Though seven times, or seventy times seven,
Your armies circle our beleaguered town,
Not with their clamor may our gates be riven;
O, not by trumpets shall the walls go down!
Send out your troops to trample the fresh grasses
With horns and banners! They shall find defeat.
These walls can bear the insolence of brasses
Sounded at noonday in the dust and heat.

It is the whisper, only, that we dread:
The hushed and delicate murmur like low weeping
Which shall assail us, when, as do the dead,
The warders sleep and all the town lies sleeping.
That holy word is whispered which can fell
These armored walls, and raze the citadel.

Six Nuns in the Snow

Beautifully, now, they walk among these new
petals the snow shook down—
identical figures, going two by two,
each in a black gown.

With what a placid tread, what definite,
calm impulse each proceeds,
two by two, black on bewildering white,
swinging her long beads;

an absolute six, taking their candid way
undazzled by this whiteness,
who have grown used to walking without dismay
amid incredible brightness.

Portrait

Her thought is separate from her act
    And neither her defender is,
Whose nature seems at once compact
    Of courage and of cowardice.

Beset by hurricane and flood,
    She seeks no amnesty from Death,
Yet lacks intrinsic hardihood
    To weather a disdainful breath.

Watching the year grow late, grow late,
    She finds no desperation in it,
But cannot bear love's little wait
    Between a minute and a minute.

Let the earth shake. She stands her ground.
    Let her house fall. She will not flee,
Who yet is shattered by the sound
    Of one door, closing, distantly.

Intimations of Mortality

On being told by the dentist that "this will be over soon"

Indeed, it will soon be over, I shall be done
  With the querulous drill, the forceps, the clove-smelling cotton.
I can go forth into fresher air, into sun,
  This narrow anguish forgotten.

In twenty minutes or forty or half an hour,
  I shall be easy, and proud of my hard-got gold.
But your apple of comfort is eaten by worms, and sour.
  Your consolation is cold.

This will not last, and the day will be pleasant after.
  I'll dine tonight with a witty and favorite friend.
No doubt tomorrow I shall rinse my mouth with laughter.
  And also that will end.

The handful of time that I am charily granted
  Will likewise pass, to oblivion duly apprenticed.
Summer will blossom and autumn be faintly enchanted.
  Then time for the grave, or the dentist.

Because you are shrewd, my man, and your hand is clever,
  You must not believe your words have a charm to spell me.
There was never a half of an hour that lasted forever.
  Be quiet. You need not tell me.

ON THE TOWN

Valentine for New York

Moscow is Red, Pittsburgh is gritty.
I know a nicer kind of city.
It's on the Hudson, not the Rhine.
Manhattan, be my valentine.

Tumultuous town, absurd and thunderful,
I think you're wonderful—
Sleeping or waking, frivolous or stable,
Down at the heel, or opulent in sable,
I like your voices, single or together.
I even like your weather
(Your rains, your wind that down the river blows,
Your heat, your fogs, your perishable snows).
I like your pomp and civic ceremony.
I like you real. I love you when you're phony.
In other words, no matter where I gad about,
You're what I'm mad about.

Then stay with me and be my dear,
  Accept this honest flattery,
And I will sing your praises, clear
  From Harlem to the Battery.

I sing the Empire State that magnates dwell in.
I sing Sixth Avenue without the "L" in,

Bedraggled square and screaming boulevard,
And Mr. Morgan's elegant back yard.
I sing St. Thomas's, which sponsors marriages.
I sing your parks equipped with lads and wenches,
With dogs on leashes, and with tots in carriages
And men on wooden benches.
I sing the penthouse, harboring your élite,
And four-flight walkups snug on Barrow Street;
Your native cops, more virile than the bobby,
And Powers models and the Astor lobby.

I sing your Automats,
Your gentle tearooms, wary of the scallion;
The Colony, where wend the risible hats,
And tables d'hôte excessively Italian;
And ferryboats and boogie-woogie bands
And Nedick Orange stands.

Metropolis, aloud I praise
Your febrile nights, your clamorous days.
Not even the sales tax, trying hard,
Can cut in two my deep regard.

Be mine, be mine:
Shop, subway, danceteria, picket line;
The Planetarium, replete with stars;
Buses and banks and débutante bazaars;
And traffic lights reflected, when it rains,
In all the pavements; and the skiing trains;
Orchids by Schling and men in areaways
Selling bouquets;
The show that sells out and the one that closes;
Auctions, and all the deeds of Mr. Moses,
And Sunday bells, and pretty secretaries
Eating their lunch at soda stands or dairies;
Progressive schools that cope with Freudian symbols,
And monasteries selling cheap at Gimbels;
Jaywalkers, and St. Patrick's Day parades;
And part-time maids,

And art museums, where I take my aunts;
And Mott Street, and the Ballroom Renaissance,
Where sound the brasses that the dancers spin to;
And El Morocco, which I've never been to;
And kitchenettes and pubs,
And Kansas clubs;
The elms at Radio City, spreading tall;
Foghorns, and pigeons—yes, and Tammany Hall.

Let others, finding flaw or pointing fault,
Accept you with their cautious grains of salt.
Egregious city, facing toward the sea,
Abide with me.

Boston's well bred, Philadelphia's Blue.
Borough of Manhattan, I love you.

Monday Is Fish Day

On Monday mornings early, before the town is shrill,
When the dew is on the milkman and the bacon's on the grill,
I hurry to the doorstep, intent upon my mission
To read if Curator Christopher Coates
   Has made the first edition.

       For six days a week
       The *Times* talks of treaties,
       The *Tribune* damns the Democrats
          With many a tosh and pish,
       But nothing happens Sunday,
       So happily on Monday
       Reporters get the story
          Of Mr. Coates's fish.

When nations keep the Sabbath, when all the world relaxes
From wars and litigation and armament and taxes,

Then who can save the papers, their presses stricken dumb,
Save only Curator Christopher Coates
   At the City Aquarium?

      For six days a week
      There's a panic or a killing,
      On six days a week
        There are courts to abuse,
      But Sunday is a flat day.
      Nothing happens *that* day,
      So every Monday morning
        Mr. Coates supplies the news.

Then down with Thursday's scandal, with Wednesday's scoop,
    away!
Throw out the double murder assigned for Saturday.
I wait the throbbing headline that Monday morn reveals
When Mr. Curator Christopher Coates
   Discusses tropic eels.

      I raise up a cheer
      For goldfish and guppies,
      And print the kiss of honor
        On Mr. Coates's cheek,
      Who speaks when he's commanded,
      And, lone and singlehanded,
      Sustains the morning papers
        On the first of the week.

Sale Today

    What syrup, what unusual sweet,
      Sticky and sharp and strong,
  Wafting its poison through the street,
      Has lured this buzzing throng
  That swarms along the counters there
      Where bargain bait is dangled—
  Clustered like flies in honeyed snare,
      Shrill, cross, and well entangled?

Midsummer Meditations

IN FRONT OF NUMBER ONE FIFTH AVENUE

Old customs I am able
    To vision with delight,
When people sat at table
    Indoors, and out of sight;
Before the Picturesque-O
    Enslaved the urban glance,
And when to dine al fresco
    Were better done in France.

No, Cybele, that isn't a spider
In your tomato juice.

Then tearooms served your salad,
    Your cottage-cheese-and-pear,
In comfort far more valid
    Than this too-open air.
Then, safe from gawk and gaper,
    You shunned the toxic breeze,
And napkins, cloth or paper,
    Remained upon your knees.

Waiter, there's just a dash too much carbon monoxide
In the mashed potatoes.

Synthetic grass grows dusty,
    Synthetic flowers droop,
And airs of August, gusty,
    Waft cinders toward the soup.
And wearier and wearier
    Of quaintness I have grown.
Give me a dim interior
    And let me munch alone.
For I am sick of sidewalks
    Whereon to break my bread.

I simply can't abide walks
   With awnings overhead,
And forth no more I'll sally
   To where, as like as not,
They've turned a decent alley
   Into a Garden Spot.

What do you say we just stand up at the bar?

Ode to Mr. Zimmerman

At seven hundred and thirty-four
Mr. Zimmerman keeps a store
With his name in brass
On the window glass
And curtains over the door.
And a fragrant place is the corner place
Of Mr. Zimmerman's pride.
My nose goes up
Like a terrier pup
Whenever I step inside.
For coffee bubbles behind a screen,
The air is rich and murky,
And the smell to the west is still unguessed
But the northeast smell is turkey.
And the counters, the shelves, the tables, the chairs,
Are running over with beautiful wares:
Caviar, herring, and onion pickle,
Braunbrot, sauerbrot, pumpernickel,
Sweet cream patties and hard rye loaves,
Ham stuck full of spices and cloves,
And hundreds of cans enchanting me
With lithographical artistry.

I'll route my aunts to Villagish haunts
When they visit the town to see 'em.

I'll send my beau
To a musical show
And my friends to a good museum.
But I'm going down to the corner,
Insouciant as you please,
To sniff at dishes
Of pickled fishes
And little curled anchovies,
At big black olives and olives green,
Salami, schnitzel, and sardine,
Potato salad and ring of noodle,
Crumb cake, coffee cake, apple strudel!

For many a lass grows blithe and gay,
Enthralled by a Coty blending;
And jasmine under the moon, they say,
Conspires for a happy ending.
But art or nature has not contrived
A smell that ever can lessen
My constant love
For the fragrance of
The corner delicatessen;
For pears in savory sauce immersed,
Wiener sausages, liverwurst,
Stuffed tomato that no one wants,
And Roquefort cheeses and Liederkrantz,
In Mr. Zimmerman's lovely store
At seven hundred and thirty-four
With his name in brass
On the window glass,
And Plenty behind the door.

Heat Wave

These are the days democratic, the days without barriers.
Every man is a brother.
Strangers speak at the stations, at counters. In common carriers
They commiserate with each other.

Mopping their foreheads, they mutter. The walls have been leveled
That divided the sheep from the goats.
The banker wilts with his clerk. Their gear is disheveled.
They carry their coats.

Now the neat city sprawls like a village, untidy
In the smothering air.
The dazed pedestrian walks where the awnings are shady.
The legs of the ladies are bare.

Time turns like a mill wheel, slowly, but reason is wanting.
The heat is all.
(Avert your eyes from the shop windows crazily flaunting
Black satins for fall.)

The pavement sucks at the foot, the skies are ferrous,
The roofs come alive after dark.
These are the days when glasses litter the terrace
As Dixie cups the park.

And war is a tale unread while the town lolls, poring
With a masochist's delight
On the final, terrible headlines: TEMPERATURES SOARING
And NO RELIEF IN SIGHT.

Sold: to the Lady in the Green Hat

Some people spend their forces
  On mischievous games and crass.
Some people bet on horses,
  Some people love the glass.
But black as the pit from pole to pole,
  My destiny rideth clear,
For I am the wretch who's sold my soul
  To the Eloquent Auctioneer.

Silo,
  Flattau,
    Sirs at Parke-Bernet,
Somewhere an auction
  Is going on today.
And I must hie me thither
  On swift, devotional feet,
To bid 'em up
On a porcelain cup
  Or a Shakespeare (Incomplete);
To beard the hardiest Dealer
  And play him fast and loose for
A screen, a rug,
Or a Staffordshire jug
  That I haven't the slightest use for.

With bureaus the attic bulges—
  With many an antique frame;
And the shallowest drawer divulges
  Statistics of my shame.

Plaza,
  Anderson,
    Messrs. Brill & Brill!
Somewhere an auctioneer
  Is calling high and shrill.

And I must follow, follow,
   Like the tots of Hamelin town,
To spend my salary
At every gallery
   Where gentlemen knock 'em down.

All I need is a platter,
   All I want is a plate,
But I'll come back
With a magazine rack
   And a lamp that's lost its mate,
With maybe a chair and a couple of clocks
And a painted plaque and a music box
And a Minton bowl
And a casserole
And a lock-up cupboard without its locks.

For some people play at baccarat
   And some people tipple beer,
But mourn for the wretch, in muted verse,
Who's lost her head and pledged her purse
   To the Eloquent Auctioneer.

Song for an Engraved Invitation

Now, warm and sweet, the summer days
   Are opening like the rose,
With drowsy airs and languid ways
   Inviting to repose.
But not for me a green retreat
   Or any vernal asset,
Since up and down the panting street
   I stalk the demitasse set,

Or trail the silver berry spoon,
   While lunch I dare not stop for.
For what's so rare as a day in June
   Without a gift to shop for?

O June, fair June, what a month you are—
The costliest time in the calendar!
Filled, as a nettle is full of stings,
With sweet occasions for giving things.

Wherever I look, whenever I listen,
Solitaires gleam and diplomas glisten
Or babes from darkness
Emerge at Harkness
Or somebody's child is ripe to christen
Or somebody's daughter is taking a spouse
Or somebody's warming a country house
Or somebody's fledgling has finished the tenses
At Taft or Groton or maybe Spence's.

December giving strains the purse,
   December lists are grievesome.
Still, Christmas presents might be worse—
   You're certain to receive some.
But when I scurry far and wide
   Or fevered errands fly on
In search of plates to please a bride
   Or mugs to suit a scion,
I know full well that I must brood
   For solace through the summer
On pretty notes of gratitude.
   And a whacking bill from Plummer.

Sailings and weddings and births and showers!
My fate is sealed for the month of flowers.
When the first June wind blows soft and south,
I'll be looking a gift shop in the mouth.

Epithalamion

If Spenser had been on the staff of The Bride's Magazine

Hail, holy morn,
Welcome, O radiant and auspicious day!
Let every maid her person well adorn,
Let every youth go forth in cutaway.
Hail, joyous moment here at last! Unroll
The crimson carpet, brim the caterer's bowl,
Unfurl the awnings, summon without fail
The gray-gloved ushers and the groomsman pale.
Bid them be filled, e'er noon shall take its flight,
With Bromo-Seltzer and a deep delight;
And all bedight
In ascot, morning coat, and solemn looks
(Assembled jointly by the Brothers Brooks).

Come, guest and merrymaker!
Crowd the dim church, crane necks, with pride recall
How your gift (Tiffany's) outshone them all—
The carving set, the clock, the silver shaker,
The five-times duplicated crystal tumbler—
Being unique, at least, if somewhat humbler.

Now, everywhere,
Let music swell upon the happy air
In stately chords Wagnerian and slow,
While the bride's mother, she so goodly dressed
In purple chiffon, low but not too low
(And hat to match—available at Best),
Brushes away
The tear required and formal to this day.

Sound, sacred music, never cease or falter,
For cometh now the bridegroom to the altar.
How dark his eye, how splendid his cravat,
How creased his trouser and how gray his spat

(Also from Brooks), while in his coat lapel
A valley lily doth its duty well.

Even while he waits, behold, down the rich aisle,
With sweet and fixèd smile,
The bridesmaids, yellow, coral, powder blue,
Escorting Beauty's offering, and Love's,
Move altarward in rhythm, two by two
(Bonwit's ensemble, even to the gloves).

Swell louder, music! Like a blossomy bough,
It is the bride, the bride, who followeth now.
And whisper, seraphs, did you ever see
A maiden fair as she—
With step so lightsome or an eye so clear,
So tall, so slim, visaged so like a garden
(Coiffure by Antoine; skin by Elizabeth Arden),
One so attired in Skinner's super-sheer
With pleated collar and a spreading train
(Altman's design), or one with modest face
So half-obscured by veil of gauzy lace?

Ah, when she moves, there sounds a holier strain.
Now she has reached his side whose heart she weareth.
The congregation stareth,
And the hands touch, the tender vows are given.
(Prayer by the pastor; marriage—we trust—by Heaven.)

Now all is done. Bring home the bride again.
Bring home the gleesome damsels and the men
To the rich feast preparèd at the hand
Of, say, Pierre or Sherry-Netherland.
Broach the good cask, pull the embattled cork.
Let Bacchus once more revel in New York,
Bid the guests come
To drink these healths in vintages (by Mumm).
Drink to this pair made one, wake hills and highlands;
Empty your glasses, empty them and fill more.
Drink to their tickets to the Virgin Islands,
Drink to their luggage (straight from Arthur Gilmore),

And let the welkin ring
Toasting their dovecote (plans by Bing & Bing).
Yea, call a blessing down
Upon this happiest pair in all the town.
May only joy be theirs, all things delight them,
Nor Reno nor a budget e'er affright them.
Prosperity be theirs, and friends, and health,
And relatives to leave them all their wealth.
Kind spirits hover round this bride's dear head.
Give her a full-time maid to call her own,
Charge accounts, and a private telephone.
And scatter pleasure o'er the marriage bed!
(Mattress by Simmons; bed by W. and J. Sloane.)

Song to Be Sung After Labor Day

Bring in the blue October skies,
    Bring in the autumn weather,
For the frost upon the pumpkin lies
    And the wild geese fly together.
The wild geese fly together now,
    To sunnier climates wending,
And I shall lay my bags away
    And go no more week-ending.

To flower and field I'll say farewell,
    Farewell the round-trip ticket.
I leave the farmer in the dell,
    The bramble in the thicket.
The trains may come, the trains may go,
    Long Island or New Haven,
But I shall bide by my fireside,
    In comfort deep and craven.

No more, with luggage laden down,
I'll leave the snug, the tranquil town,

For windy hills or tossing breakers
Or someone's poison-ivied acres.
On my own couch I'll take my slumber,
With bedclothes adequate in number,
Whence I'll arise when day impels me,
And not that hour my hostess tells me.
Yes, I'll be Luxury's favorite daughter,
My bathroom tap will run hot water,
The alien towel I'll cry no pox on,
I'll have some hooks to hang my frocks on,
I'll fear no spate of extra women,
Nor weedy pools dammed up to swim in.
My mind will rest, my mind will harden,
I'll seek no words to praise a garden,
I will not picnic with a hamper
Where grass is damp and boughs are damper,
Nor by a brook, nor in a meadow,
Nor where the bonfire crackles red. Oh,
Neat and safe upon a chair,
I will not picnic anywhere.

No more I'll rack my desperate brains
     For gifts to show my gratitude,
Nor ponder wells and roofs and drains
     With revential attitude.
For trains may come and trains may go,
     The Central or the Erie,
But I shall hug my own hearthrug
     And, if I will, be dreary.

Turn back the daylight-saving clock,
     Bed down in urban clover!
For the fodder's rusting in the shock
     And the week-end season's over.

Incident on Madison Avenue

On Saturday, amid the crowd
   That in the sunshine drifted by,
I wandered happy as a cloud
   Afloat with fellow-cumuli,
Till suddenly, and face to face,
I came on Mr. Morgan's place.

On Mr. Morgan's house I came,
   Where wonder brought me to a standstill.
The iron gates were yet the same,
   The gardens stretched on either hand still.
But, oh, I noticed, nearly fainting,
How window sills cried out for painting.

As shabby and as weather-beat
   As those of mortgage-bearing biped,
The sashes shamed that shining street;
   They were not even washed and wipèd.
And, staring on that sight appalling,
I felt the world around me falling.

Upon my ears the tumbrels sounded,
   While wealth decayed and Fortune groaned.
I looked on Privilege, surrounded,
   The Mighty from their seats dethroned.
And quick, in terror and abasement,
I fled each drear, unpainted casement.

Now, hidden from the curious gapers,
   I weep and know the end is near.
I have not dared to read the papers,
   Lest they should tell me what I fear:
That mine and Wall Street's Patron Saint
Cannot afford a can of paint.

Short History of Cooks

Dorcas broke the dishes,
   Clara slumbered late,
Norah's sauces
Were total losses,
   And Sigrid stole the plate.
Mabel burnt the entrées
   And wooed the handy man,
But rich and rare
And beyond compare
   Are the works of Katharine Anne.

For Katharine Anne is a cook of cooks.
She throws away the recipe books
To bake by ear or by inspiration
And her meagrest stew is a World Sensation.
She lives to nourish the urge that's inner.
She doesn't mind if there's ten to dinner.
Lighter than foam
   Is her cheese soufflé,
And she bides at home
   When it's her off day.
On her morning coffee we call a blessing,
She doesn't put sugar in salad dressing,
Her roasts should hang in a gourmet's gallery,
And she thinks that we ought to lower her salary.

Nellie was a lady
   Who kept me in my place,
Emma's seasoning
Lacked rhyme or reasoning,
   And ennui troubled Grace.
Evangelist was Idabelle
   For starchless foods and raw,
But find who can
In Katharine Anne
   A single fault or flaw?

Oh, Katharine Anne is merry and humble.
Her cakes don't fall and her pies don't crumble,
Her custards never assail us clammily,
Our larder doesn't supply her family.
The grocery bill
   Is the bill she whittles,
She lavishes skill
   On yesterday's victuals,
Her puddings gleam like a gem from Flato's,
There are no lumps in her mashed potatoes.
She's learnèd with herbs and versed in spices,
She has no sins and she owns no vices,
She likes our kitchen, she praises her bed.
And I've made her up out of my own head.

Elegy with a Pewter Lining

How meager are the hours
   Which Grandeur may enjoy!
Gone are the gilded towers
   Whence Helen looked on Troy.
The walls are rent asunder
   Of Babylon and Rome,
And now with dust and thunder
   They raze the Hippodrome.

No more in any age, there,
   While mirth and music sound,
Will the revolving stage, there,
   Creak ponderously around
That once—so runs the story—
   Less pallid pulses stirred,
When it was all the glory
   Of 6th and 43rd.

No more will Neptune's daughters,
   Tall, languorous, and fair,

Into fantastic waters
　　Trip down a cunning stair.
To some forgotten Limbo
　　The elephants depart,
That ere the time of Jumbo
　　Won plaudits for their art.

Gone now each stately Juno
　　Robed like the Evening Star.
Gone even the airs from Gounod
　　At prices popular.
Yet, lest we mourn forever
　　Old, fabulous delights—
The comic's grim endeavor,
　　The spangles and the tights,

The tumblers in formation,
　　The Death-Defying Dive—
Take this for consolation:
　　Still do the pageants thrive.
Disguised with newer fashions,
　　Still, still, the Turns are played,
Since now the Paid Admissions
　　Can watch the Aquacade.

For never blows
So red and hot and splendid
The Billy Rose
As when some epoch's ended.

November

Away with vanity of Man.
　Now comes to visit here
The Maiden Aunt, the Puritan,
　The Spinster of the year.

She likes a world that's furnished plain,
　A sky that's clean and bare,
And garments eminently sane
　For her consistent wear.

Let others deck them as they please
　In frill and furbelow.
She scorns alike the fripperies
　Of flowers and of snow.

Her very speech is shrewd and slight,
　With innuendoes done;
And all of her is hard, thin light
　Or shadow sharp as sun.

Indifferent to the drifting leaf,
　And innocent of guile,
She scarcely knows there dwells a brief
　Enchantment in her smile.

So love her with a sparing love.
　That is her private fashion,
Who fears the August ardor of
　A demonstrated passion.

Yet love her somewhat. It is meet,
　And for our own defense,
After October to find sweet
　Her chilly common sense.

Dirge over a Pot of Pâté de Foie Gras

"The present chairman of the board, William A. Charles, a son of one of the founders, has no heir to carry on the name and has decided to retire. Neither is there a male heir in the family of Archibald C. Charles, which also holds an interest in the business."
—*News item from the* New York Herald Tribune.

Weep for an empire falling.
   Weep for a lost endeavor.
Cry ruin and woe,
Since Charles & Co.
   Has bolted its doors forever.
Let sobs be broken, let tears be saline.
Charles & Company has no male line.

Not that the Trade had left them.
   Not for a worldly reason
Are the cupboards locked
And the shelves unstocked
   With succulence out of season.
A cause more sad and a lack more germinal
Has dimmed that glory beside the Terminal.

For where are the sons of Charles's,
   Heirs to the founding sires?
Who shall be lord
Of the Governing Board
   When William A. retires?
How shall a company sell or buy on,
When feminine is its seed and scion?

The epicures keen in concert,
   The gourmet averts his glance.
Gone like a wind
Are the puddings, tinned,
   And the vintages out of France.
Gone the caviar, gone the truffles,
Banished by daughterly skirts and ruffles.

Gone from those splendid counters
   That watered the mouth of yore
Are the jams
And the hams
And the teas
And the cheese;
The grand things,
The canned things,
The stuffed and the potted,
The savory bits
That our wits besotted;
The soup-with-sherry,
The wild strawberry,
The bacon taken
From Cork or Kerry,
And all of the viands
That ever made merry
   Our fanciest grocery store.
Swathed are the Baskets in crepe and tissue,
For Charles & Co. has no male issue.

Evening Musicale

Candles. Red tulips, ninety cents the bunch.
   Two lions, Grade B. A newly tuned piano.
No cocktails, but a dubious kind of punch,
   Lukewarm and weak. A harp and a soprano.
The "Lullaby" of Brahms. Somebody's cousin
   From Forest Hills, addicted to the pun.
Two dozen gentlemen; ladies, three dozen,
   Earringed and powdered. Sandwiches at one.

The ash trays few, the ventilation meager.
   Shushes to greet the late-arriving guest
Or quell the punch-bowl group. A young man eager
   To render "Danny Deever" by request.
And sixty people trying to relax
On little rented chairs with gilded backs.

Lament

*Upon learning that Grover Whalen is no longer listed
among the nation's best-dressed men*

Mourn, city of boroughs and bridges,
Wail, desolate town.
To the dust, to the ants and the midges
Your grandeurs go down.
The tailors have spoken. An age that was splendid
Is ended.

That glossy perfection which blossomed more rich than the rose
From official tonneaus;
That artful ensemble which dazzled the gaping beholder—
The accurate Shoulder,
The Pocket, restrainèd but swell,
The lordly Lapel,
The fawn-colored Glove, the Cravat,
The Spat—
To oblivion slide. They have raised up the drab and the flighty
To the seats of the mighty.

Now, wardrobes expansive but menial
Depose the regalia gardenial.
The trousers whose crease was a creed
Give way to the slovenly tweed;
While the elegant topper,
The Chesterfield, fitted and proper,
Have both come a cropper.
And amateur raiment in Mass. or the middling West
Is crowned as the best.

Oh, therefore, while Dignity keens
At a blow that is crushing,
Weep! Brooklyn, Manhattan, and Queens,
Especially Flushing.

Let touring celebrities heavy of head and of heart
Amid their confetti depart.
Let cameras hide in their coverts, reporters be humble,
Let cornerstones crumble.
The tailors have spoken. The glory of Grover
Is over.

Enigma in Altman's

It is a strange, miraculous thing
    About department stores,
How elevators upward wing
    By twos and threes and fours,

How pale lights gleam, how cables run
    All day without an end,
Yet how reluctant, one by one,
    The homing cars descend.

They soar to Furniture, or higher,
    They speed to Gowns and Gifts,
But when the bought weighs down the buyer,
    Late, late, return the lifts.

Newton, himself, beneath his tree,
    Would ponder this and frown:
How what goes up so frequently
    So seldom cometh down.

Song from New Rochelle

Monday's child is fair of face,
    And her driver's a handsome fellow.
Tuesday's child is full of grace,
    So she gracefully hails a Yellow.
Wednesday's child has a red coupé,
    With a little black horn she toots.
But I was born on a Saturday,
    And Saturday's child commutes!

CHORUS

No responsibility is assumed for errors in timetables
Nor for inconvenience or damage resulting from delayed trains
Or failure to make connections.

They that live on Washington Square
    May sleep as long as they please.
And they slumber deep and they slumber fair
    In the affluent Seventies.
In Tudor City the good and mild
    Lie late with a brow serene.
But I am only Saturday's child
    So I get the eight-sixteen.

CHORUS

Buy tickets before boarding trains, and avoid
Payment of extra charge.

The other girls go out to play
    In the fields of corn and clover.
And the other girls can always stay
    Until the party's over.
But just when the height is at its fun
    And the yodeler's growing vocal,
I am the one who needs must run
    To catch the Stamford local.

It's I whom hostesses yearn to shelve;
   The Bridge-Table Blight am I.
(If Cinderella went home at twelve,
   She probably lived in Rye.)
Before the chorus has ceased to smile
   Or the maestro dropped his baton,
I am the lass in the middle aisle
   Who's trying to get her hat on.

Oh, gaiety dwells
In the best hotels,
   But little to me it boots.
For I was born
On Saturday morn
   And Saturday's child commutes.

CHORUS

The schedules shown herein are subject
To change without notice.

THE HOUSE OF OLIVER AMES

Apology for Husbands

*In answer to a friend's observation that they're
"more bother than they're worth"*

Although your major premise, dear,
    Is rather sharp than subtle,
My honest argument, I fear,
    Can offer scant rebuttal.

I grant the Husband in the Home
    Disrupts its neat machinery.
His shaving brush, his sorry comb,
    Mar tidy bathroom scenery.

When dinner's prompt upon the plate,
He labors at the office late;
Yet stay him while the stew is peppered,
He rages like a famished leopard.
He rages like an angry lion
When urged to put a formal tie on,
But should festivities grow hearty,
He is the last to leave the party.
He lauds your neighbor's giddy bonnet
But laughs, immoderate, if you don it,
And loathes your childhood friend, and always
Bestrews his garments through the hallways.

But e'er you shun the wedded male,
    Recall his special talents
For driving firm the picture nail
    And coaxing books to balance.

Regard with unalloyed delight
    That skill, which you were scorning,
For opening windows up at night
    And closing them at morning.

Though under protest, to be sure,
He weekly moves the furniture.
He layeth rugs, he fixeth sockets,
He payeth bills from both his pockets.
For invitations you decry
He furnisheth an alibi.
He jousts with taxi-men in tourney,
He guards your luggage when you journey,
And brings you news and quotes you facts
And figures out the income tax
And slaughters spiders when you daren't
And makes a very handy parent.

What gadget's useful as a spouse?
    Considering that a minute,
Confess that every proper house
    Should have a husband in it.

A Marriage of Convenience

Now whom did Oliver lean on,
    Before we two were wed,
To remind him, say,
On the natal day
    Of his affluent Uncle Fred?
Who wrote the news
    To his friends and folks?

Who gave him the cues
   For his favorite jokes?
Who scribbled his greetings when cards were sent out?
Who counted his collars before they went out?
Who hung up his racquets and stored his putter
And thanked his hosts for their bread and butter?

Whose eagle eye was alert to spy
   The sag in his trousers' creases?
With vision and thrift
Who bought the gift
   For the nuptials of his nieces?
Who dusted his satchel,
   Who packed his cases,
When he was a bachel-
   Or, going places?
For invitations he couldn't condone,
Who gave his regrets on the telephone?
And bundled him up for rain or mist
And checked the names on his Christmas list?

Yes, who ran Oliver's errands,
   Busily, sun to sun?
Or gave him warning
To rise at morning,
   Before we twain were one?
Of his kith and kin,
   He was wary, very.
And it couldn't have been
   His secretary,
And never an angel and not an elf.
So perhaps it was Oliver Ames, himself.
But I say it's odd how my legal lord
Has thrown those worriments overboard.

For it's needles and pins,
But a fig for father.
When a man marries
He just doesn't bother.

Oliver Meets an Emergency

Cry storm, cry stress from every casement.
There's devastation in the basement;
There's havoc loose amid the plumbing.
But hark! Do I hear rescue coming?

Yes, aid we need no further seek, now
For Oliver will mend that leak, now.
Rebellious drains that threaten plaster
Have met for once their lord and master.

Then rally round, you helpers fluttery.
Rally from kitchen, bath and buttery.
Ring up your friends, call in the neighbors
To help our hero at his labors.

Bring him his gloves and leather jerkin.
Bring overalls for him to work in.
Bring hammers, augers, braces, bits.
Bring nails
And pails
And plumbers' kits.
Bring bulbs to light the murky distance.
(The handiest man might need assistance.)
A ladder bring,
    And tools of price,
Or anything
    Except advice.

Still flows the flood without rebuff?
You'd best keep right on bringing stuff.
Bring coffee (black). Bring milk and sandwiches.
Bring iodine and sterile bandwiches.
Bring sympathy. Bring groans and tears.
Bring cotton wool to stop your ears

When syllables grow terse and torrid.
Bring handkerchiefs to wipe his forehead.

Bring someone's thumb to hold the dike.
Bring brooms, bring mops. And if you'd like
This pipe repaired before it's summer,
Perhaps you'd better bring the plumber.

Motto to Be Framed in a Guest Room

Some folk they say
At break of day
   Ecstatically awaken
And straightway rise
With joyful cries
   To sniff the rashered bacon.
Their hearts are light, their heads are clear,
   For repartee they're able,
And neatly buttoned they appear
   Each morning at the table.
Well, doubtless they're a worthy crew,
   More potent than a powerhouse.
But God forbid that they should do
   Their breakfasting at our house.

For hark,
The lark
At heaven's gate
   Like Lily Pons may warble—
The clan of Ames
Morosely claims
   There is no bird so horr'ble.
The rosy dawn delights us not.
   We view the sun with loathing,
While staggering from reluctant cot
   To don distasteful clothing.

Two figures bowed with haste and gloom,
    Daring the day to flower,
Each glares at each across the room
    And stumbles to the shower.

Oh, chill, forlorn,
Unholy morn
    The Ames were never friend to!
With dull accord
The breakfast board
    We drearily descend to.
No gladsome quips
Escape our lips.
    In epithets we mutter,
Or beg at most
The plate of toast
    Or snarl above the butter.
And we must drain the Java's dregs
And quaff the juice and crack the eggs
And find the energy to stuff in
A second cup, another muffin,
Before conceding that we may
As well exist another day.

Yes, some folk rise
With starry eyes
    When dawn's a kindling ember.
But here's a warning and a clue.
Till breakfast's positively through,
The Ameses can't be spoken to.
    And we'll thank you to remember.

Don't Write, Wire

*A poem composed after attending an exhibition of
the love letters of the poets*

Oliver Ames is a gentleman of
   Qualities wise and witty.
And Oliver Ames, my own true love,
   Has journeyed to Salt Lake City,
Whence each day (as I swore he'd better)
He sends me a lyrically worded letter
That throbs with ardor and pulses with passion
In somewhat the following fervent fashion:

> *Darling, I've just*
>   *A minute or two,*
> *But I simply must*
>   *Get off to you*
> *A dutiful note as I said I would.*
> *I haven't been feeling so very good.*
> *The boys, here, threw me a little revel,*
> *And my head aches now like the very devil.*
> *The weather is fine and I wish you were*
> *Here.   Love.*
>   *Hastily,*
>
>   *Oliver*

For Oliver Ames, my all-in-all,
   Clever at How and When To,
Is hardly ever poetical
   In letters he puts his pen to.
So, disappointed, taking it hard,
I hurried out with a library card
To feast my mind on the missives planned
By poets, taking their quills in hand.
Among my betters
   I sought my wish
I read the letters
   Of Percy Bysshe.

I peeped at Poe in the common mail,
And Johnson writing to Mrs. Thrale,
Thackeray, Longfellow, Bobbie Burns—
All the gentlemen served their turns.
And these are the amorous works of art
With whose old sweetness I fed my heart:

> *Dearest Mary,*
> *So Shelley wrote,*
> *I've time for the very*
> *Briefest note.*
> *But I am well and I hope you're so.*
> *Here is the coach and I'd better go.*
> *Love.*
> *P. Shelley.*

      O, Hail, Blithe Spirit!
That's what you said, or something near it.
And Robert Burns when he wrote his dear
Railed at too many mugs of beer
For the boys had given a little revel
And his head ached then like the very devil.
Boswell cried that his horse was winner,
Thackeray ardently hymned his dinner,
And Dr. Johnson with classic phrase
Sighed of nostrums that filled his days.
He spoke of pains in his legs and back
And listed the virtues of ipecac.

For Oliver Ames, my bosom's staff,
   Whenever it's his ambition
To put out a palpitant paragraph,
   Falls heir to a great tradition.
The hands are wrung and the lips are bitten
But the sentiment never gets really written.

And he and Shelley and all the others
Under the skin, in this, are brothers.

Recipe for a Marriage

WITH A CURTSY TO MR. BURNS

John Anderson my jo, John,
    When we were first acquaint,
I had a fault or so, John,
    And you were less than saint.
But once we'd said a brave "I do"
    And paid the parson's fee,
I set about reforming you
    And you reforming me.

John Anderson my jo, John,
    Our years have journeyed fair;
I think, as couples go, John,
    We've made a pleasant pair.
For us, contented man and wife,
    The marriage bond endures,
Since you have changed my way of life
    And I have altered yours.

Let captious people say, John,
    There's poison in that cup.
We found a simple way, John,
    To clear each difference up.
We could not swap our virtues, John,
    So this was our design:
All your bad habits I took on,
    While you adopted mine.
Until the final lightnings strike,
    It's comfortable to know
Our faults we share and share alike,
    John Anderson my jo.

View from a Suburban Window

When I consider how my light is spent,
   Also my sweetness, ditto all my power,
Papering shelves or saving for the rent
   Or prodding grapefruit while the grocers glower,
Or dulcetly persuading to the dentist
   The wailing young, or fitting them for shoes,
Beset by menus and my days apprenticed
   Forever to a grinning household muse;

And how I might, in some tall town instead,
   From nine to five be furthering a Career,
   Dwelling unfettered in my single flat,
My life my own, likewise my daily bread—
   When I consider this, it's very clear
   I might have done much worse. I might, at that.

Love in the Depression

Pity all lovers who for love awaken
To desolation, and forlorn are bedded—
The thrust apart by malice, the forsaken,
And those whose dears are dust or false or wedded.
Look with compassion on the ones who sicken
With the old malady that Dido knew;
That same whereby Verona's pair was stricken,
And Hero and Elaine. But pity, too,

The luckless brood, this generation's litter,
For whom the flower shows a hopeful petal
That poverty must wither, and the bitter
Wind of delay; who see their love's good metal
Moment by moment darken to their gaze
In the dank air of these corroding days.

Trinity Place

The pigeons that peck at the grass in Trinity Churchyard
  Are pompous as bankers. They walk with an air, they preen
Their prosperous feathers. They smugly regard their beauty.
They are plump, they are sleek. It is only the men who are lean.

The pigeons scan with disfavor the men who sit there,
    Listless in sun or shade. The pigeons sidle
Between the gravestones with shrewd, industrious motions.
    The pigeons are busy. It is only the men who are idle.
The pigeons sharpen their beaks on the stones, and they waddle
    In dignified search of their proper, their daily bread.
Their eyes are small with contempt for the men on the benches.
    It is only the men who are hungry. The pigeons are fed.

Progress

*"Scientists declare grass contains more vitamins than all other fruits
and vegetables put together."*   —*News item in the* New York Times.

Nebuchadnezzar, snug in Hell,
    But panting still in that fervid clime,
Read the papers and sighed, "How dull
    To have been a prophet before one's time!

"I ranged the meadows beside the cattle,
    I fed on the fields to atone my sins,
And no one knew I had found a subtle
    Method of getting my vitamins.

"Had I been born to a later people,"
    Cried Babylon's King, "Alack, alas,
How many an eager and lean disciple
    Had followed me out to the living grass!

"Then, roving naked amid the stubble,
    Half a nation on hand and knee
Would worry the lawns and champ and nibble
    Or name an Institute after me."

Ordeal by Family

I've been out where the Blues begin,
Stopping at home with my kith and kin,
Where the handclasp's firm, and the smile is humorous,
And Family Friends are a bit too numerous.

    Oh, Family Friends are staunch and sound.
        Their virtues all are double.
    Family Friends, they rally round
        Whenever you're in trouble.
    Family Friends are worth their weight
        In any goods you carry.
    But they incline to speculate
        On when you're going to marry.

Family Friends, if they're feminine,
Wear their chins in a triple line.
Or, if of masculine gender, they
Have positive views on the NRA.

    Oh, Family Friends will fight for you
        To the utmost ditch.
    Family Friends are loyal and true,
        Sometimes even rich.
    But Family Friends are apt to fret
        About your squandered wages.
    And lest you haply might forget,
        They always mention ages.

Oh, Family Friends sit round in a ring
And give you counsel on everything.
They think red nails are an incongruity.
They urge you to buy a good annuity.
Their smiles are kind and their eyes are mild.
They want to fatten you up, poor child,
And feed you lovely chicken-and-waffley
Meals designed to upset you awfully.

They say "How tragic!" and "What a pity!"
And of your life in the fervid city,
They ask in an interested kind of way
But never listen to what you say.

   Oh, Family Friends are noble folk,
     With noble views on life.
   Each husband tells his little joke,
     Applauded by his wife.
   All the men are gentlemen,
     The ladies more than such.
   And now that I'm away again,
     I miss them very much.

Apostrophe to a Nephew

Up, lovely infant, rosy sib,
   Up, vigorous embracer!
Cast down the rattle, loose the bib.
Oh, shame, to linger in your crib!
   You're ten months old today, sir.
Ten moons on you have waxed and waned.
   Survey the time you've squandered,
Boarded and bedded, entertained,
   And all too often laundered,
The while your playmates and your peers,
   Your very generation,
Are carving for themselves careers
   That stir the startled nation.

In concert halls, on silver screens,
   They win the country over.
Their mothers ride in limousines,
Their dads have money in their jeans,
   Their aunts reside in clover.
The land is full of prodigies
   With flannel round their middles.

They pound upon piano keys,
  They lean upon their fiddles,
They sparkle up at cameramen
  (If fat enough their parts are).
Their wage is as the wage of ten
  Because so pure their hearts are.

Yet does your young ambition burn?
  Is industry your habit?
Ah, no—your present whole concern
  Is one white woollen rabbit.
You might be sending on the air
  That well-rehearsèd bellow.
You might be practicing with care
  The chessboard or the 'cello.
You might be posing in the nude
  On contract signed and juicy.
You might be sponsoring Baby Food
  Or rendering Debussy.
You might, at least, improvident kin,
  If you'd acquired forbearance,
Be writing little verses in
  Connection with your parents.

So, chubby charmer, up, I say,
  And lisp your way to power!
For you are ten months old today
  And now's the Children's Hour,
When ancestors may gather all
  The rights that are decreed them.
Cast down the rattle, drop your ball,
And read upon your nursery wall
  How a little child shall feed them.

The Kingdom and the Glory

"Count Curt Haugwitz-Reventlow and his wife, the former Barbara Hutton Mdivani, are en route to London for the Coronation. Two governesses and a nurse are in attendance on Lance, their baby son."
—*News item.*

"Boom," say the cannons, and "Hail," sing the banners,
"Ho," cry the heralds with their elegantest manners.
"Here comes a Sovereign to greet a brother king—
A little prince chewing on a teething ring!"

> High street, low street,
>   Parliament Square
> Send a rousing welcome
>   To the Woolworth heir!
> Greet him, every horseman,
>   In plume and shining button.
> His father is a Norseman,
>   His mother was a Hutton.

Here comes the Scion, as regal as can be,
With henchmen and footmen and handmaidens three,
To comfort him with mittens and cut his spinach up,
And feed him his gruel from a monogrammed cup.

> Three ladies haughty
>   To lean above his crib,
> To spank him when he's naughty,
>   And tie the royal bib;
> To teach him pretty answers
>   And zip his zippers ùndone.
> Young Count Lance, sirs,
>   Is on his way to London.

Merry ring the church bells, loud play the bands,
Proud ride the monarchs with their scepters in their hands.

And some fear the Fascists and some dread the Debt,
But Lance goes smiling in his bassinet.

High street, low street,
    Wish the Infant joy!
Lift a rousing welcome
    To the last Royal Boy.
For empires daily totter,
    And princes sulk in Rome,
And a king across the water
    Awaits the mail from home.
But the pillow's made of down,
    And the head lies easy when
It's a head that wears a crown
    From the Five-and-Ten.

Lines in Praise of Our National Capital

Composed while waiting for a green light

O, I have been to the Capital, and it's there I'd end my days,
    Where the Judas tree is flowering now and the dogwood lifts
    its crown;
Where the fauna and flora and Senator Borah attract the passing
    gaze,
    And it's twenty cents for a taxicab to any place in town!

O, I have been to the Capital, where the D. A. R. convene,
    (Their bosoms are built on the Lane Bryant plan, and they
    favor armaments),
Where party quarrel and mountain laurel enrich the public scene,
    And I rode five miles in a taxicab and it cost me twenty cents!

Then ho! for the beautiful D. of C. where our leaders guard and
    guide us.
    I'm going to live in the Capital and leave this life so drab.
I'll weep no more as the meters soar, but nonchalant as Midas,
    For twenty cents I'll ride around in a Diamond Taxicab!

Star-Spangled Ode

My country, 'tis to thee and all thy ways
I lift my harp in praise.
Land of tall forests, hills, lakes, seas, and valleys
(The Pilgrims' pride and likewise the O'Malleys'),
Haven to heroes from oppression fleeting
(Viz: Kosciusko, Thomas Mann, and Erika);
Country of canyons, corn, and central heating,
    Of thee I sing, America!

While statesmen fume and bicker in thy name,
    Thunder upon the Left or damn the Tories,
My task shall be, unblushing, to proclaim
    Thy singular, matchless, and immoderate glories.

        Hail, Columbia, happy spot,
        Gem of a double ocean.
        Here I, embattled patriot,
        Publish my stout devotion.

Hail, birthplace of my Gramp.
    Hail customs, monuments, cities, paths, and byways;
Each garden, farm, park, house, and tourist camp,
    And every trailer on your teeming highways.
Hail, land that loved the French and fought the Hessian,
    That dreamed of unearned riches, like Aladdin;
Place of the Uplift, and the graphed Recession,
    Charlie McCarthy, and Bernarr Macfadden;

That in your ample bosom can enclose
Pikes Peak and Billy Rose,
New England lilacs fragrant where you pass,
And the gold poppy in the Western grass.

For good or ill, this is my chosen nation,
    Home of Joe Louis and the D.A.R.,

Fairs, floods, the Federal Investigation,
    And the used car;
Cape Cod, the Coca-Cola, Mount Rainier,
    The Swanee River and the River Bronx,
The Dies Committee and the roasting ear,
    And Scottish songs in swing time at the On'x;
Of rocking chairs on country porches rocking,
And the slim leg in the superlative stocking.

All these do I rejoice in with rejoicing:
    Jones Beach, blueberry pie, and mocking birds,
And Mrs. Doctor Mayo, sweetly voicing
    American Motherhood's authentic words;
And footballs in October attitudes.
And Automats, and packaged breakfast foods.
Now more and evermore
Dear to my heart is this, my native shore,
Where Liberty lingers still, and even Hope
Unvanquished dwells;
Where dentists ply their trade, and there is soap—
Soap, and hot waters steaming, in hotels.
Where none so humble or his lot so low
But in his house there blares the Radio.

> *Oh, beautiful for spacious skies*
>   *And waving fields of grain,*
> *For everything a buyer buys*
>   *Embalmed in Cellophane.*
> *America, America,*
>   *I call each prospect good,*
> *From Maryland*
> *To the Goldwyn strand*
>   *Of shining Hollywood.*

What do we lack that other nations boast of?
    What splendor or what plague?
Unanimous Italy may make the most of
    Her Duce. We have Hague.

As favorably our plains and mountains size up;
    Our suns are brighter and our snows as chill,
And more profusely do our billboards rise up
    On every templed hill.
And if, beneath the tread of iron heels,
Our earth less sickly reels,
    Where are the armies valianter than these—
Our troops of marching boys assembling yet,
Lads without uniform or bayonet,
    Who come to grips with trees?
And we have Donald Duck and Passamaquoddy,
And more laws than *any*body.

EPILOGUE

Now dies upon my ear
    The eagle screaming and the hollow cheer,
The politician's loud and public tone,
And the La Follette calling to its own.
Only I hear
Above the din, the clamor, the stone-flinging,
Freedom, yet faintly ringing.

And by the dawn's dim light I see you stand,
O indestructible land,
Swaggering still, and binding up your hurts,
    Building your towers, digging impossible ditches;
Your leaders clad in ordinary shirts,
    Your Kennedy clinging to his common britches.
So that I cry, secure within your gates,
O.K., United States.

The Further Off from England . . .

"Grace Moore says controversy rages in Cannes over her curtsy to the Duchess of Windsor, with the Countess of Pembroke, etiquette authority, leading the opposition."   —Headline in the New York Post.

"Will you move a little faster?" said the Diva to the Duke.
"There's a Countess close behind me and she's dealing out rebuke.
Won't you please persuade your Family to employ the final mercy,
For the Côte d'Azur is crackling in the flames of Controversy.
Your lady's name is ancient,
    But her blood is somewhat newer.
So shall we, shan't we, shall we, shan't we,
    Shall we curtsy to her?

"I bowed to you, I bowed to her, I bent the full degree.
I sent a chilling shudder through the British Colony.
A Peeress sought her pallet and a Peer got indigestion,
And Cannes is split in twain about a Very Vital Question.
Casinos hum with gossip,
    And villas surge with strife,
For can we, can't we, can we, can't we
    Recognize your wife?

"In other lands and countries, on less amazing shores,
They talk of pacts and politics and armaments and wars.
They babble over treaties or vilify the Debt,
But on the Riviera we are torn by Etiquette.
All furrowed are our foreheads,
    Considering the case
Of may we, might we, may we, might we
    Curtsy to Her Grace."

"Ah, well the earth may tremble and well the world may rock,"
Said the Singer to reporters when they met her at the dock.
"For who can eat his caviar and who can slumber sound
When the matter to be settled is a question so profound?

Along the golden beaches,
   Beside the colored sea,
Some range themselves with Pembroke
   And some line up with me.
But from no burning bush or
   Incendiary palm
Has come the final answer,
   Pontifical and calm,
To 'Does she, could she, shall she, should she
   Rate the Royal Salaam?' "

Message from Mars

"Culture is necessary, but . . . not too much of it."
       —*Virginio Gayda, editor of the Fascist* Giornale d'Italia.

Ah, what avails the sceptered race,
   And how shall fare that nation
Whose people know the evil face
   Of surplus education,
Where the unregimented lip
Is treasonable with scholarship?

Above that doomed, unblessèd land
   Shall hover like a vulture
The Democratic shadow and
   The nightmare shape of Culture,
While men of brawn and men of ink
Shall, likely, both aspire to think.

But here upon these happy shores
   Our ways shall never vary.
Though we admit
A little wit
   Is sometimes necessary,
We strike, before it rears erect,
The ugly head of Intellect;

And, free from erudition's taint,
  Our muscular Elite, O,
Shall strive from youth
To speak the truth
  As stated by Benito,
And he who follows where he's led'll
Gain the palm and win the medal.

A little language let him choose
  To read the Gospel Fascist—
A little study baiting Jew,
  Some Doctrine for the rashest,
A little War, a little Looting,
A little lesson in Saluting,
A little practice flinging down
The Bomb upon the foreign town,
A little course in shouting "Glory!"
And crying loud for Territory,
A little book-and-pamphlet burning—
But not too much of any learning.

Carol with Variations, 1936

"The world now has 7,600,000 men under arms, excluding navies, as against 5,900,000 in 1913."
  —News item printed in the New York Sun *during Christmas week.*

Oh! Little town of Bethlehem, how still we see thee lie;
Your flocks are folded in to sleep, and sleep your little ones.
Behold, there is a Star again that climbs the eastern sky.
And seven million living men are picking up their guns.

    Hark, the happy cannons roar—
    Glory to the Dictator,
    Death and fear, and peace defiled,
    And a world unreconciled!

Once more the bells of Christendom ring out a proclamation
Of joy to all the universe, and mercy, and good will;
While brother shoots his brother down, and nation scowls at nation,
And seven million uniforms are decorate at drill.

Hail to Dupont and to Krupp!
Steel is strong and going up.
Let the tidings glad be sent—
'Tis the Morn of Armament.

God rest you merry, gentlemen, whose will these armies are.
Go proudly in your colored shirts, let nothing you dismay.
(Oh, little town of Bethlehem, how fades your shining star?)
While seven million fighting men stand up on Christmas Day.

Sing hosanna, sing Noel.
Sing the gunner and the shell.
Sing the candle, sing the lamp,
Sing the Concentration Camp.
Sing the Season born anew,
Sing of exile for the Jew,
Wreathe the world with evergreen.
Praise the cunning submarine.
Sing the barbed and bitter wire,
Poison gas and liquid fire,
Bullet, bomb, and hand grenade,
And the heart of man, afraid.
Christ is come, the Light hath risen,
All our foes are safe in prison,
And the Christmastide begets
Seven million bayonets.

Hear the carol, once again—
Peace on earth, good will to men.

Wrong Formula

"I never make criticisms or comment on anything."
—Vice President Garner, as quoted in the New York Times

On matters of moment,
　　On topics political,
I never made comment,
　　I never talked critical.
When the Senate embarked
　　On unusual capers,
I seldom remarked
　　Remarks for the papers.
Though my gavel aloft
　　I would frequently swing,
My answers were soft
　　As Uvaldean Spring.
My Ire never blazed, sirs,
　　I proffered no Plan.
And everyone praised, sirs,
　　So solid a man.

Remote at the parley
　　And naming no names,
I rendered to Farley
　　The things that were James'.
Though Lending's legality
　　Filled me with grief,
I was mum on Neutrality,
　　Mute on Relief.
And, shunning pretenses,
　　While yielding my baton,
I mended my fences
　　So they could be sat on . . .
But here in my corner,
　　While argument hums,
Little Jack Garner
　　Weeps for his plums.

Ballad of the Lord and Columbus

Christopher Columbus, weary old tar—
   Fresh was the heavenly morning—
Came one day to the Judgment Bar,
   Roused by the trumpet's warning;
Rose up lightly, but with some surprise,
Looking around him and rubbing his eyes.
(For he'd done his share of toiling and of weeping
And the Lord had left him a long time sleeping.)

"Christopher Columbus," the Lord's voice spoke,
"You've had your slumber and it's time you woke.
The years are mounting,
   The centuries hum,
And every soul's accounting
   Is bound to come."
And He signed to Peter, nodding at His knee,
"Fetch the Final Record that is filed in 'C.' "

Columbus waited with a troubled look
While the Lord went thumbing through the Golden Book,
While the angels harped with suitable decorum
And the saints sat around in a haloed quorum
And the stars went whirling in an endless dance.
Said Christopher Columbus, "I'll take my chance.
A man's but human when he sails the seas,
But You know I stuck by my theories.
A queen had the credit and a king had the loot,
But I reached the Indies by the Western route."

Jehovah frowned and His voice was thunder.
"The sons of Adam, they are doomed to blunder.
Pitiful their follies of the future and the past,
But even My patience has an end at last.

You steered a passage toward the setting sun—
Regard the work that your hand has done."
(Christopher Columbus felt the heavens shake.)
"Must I forgive you for this mistake?

"I was ever vext by my peopled planet.
There's always been trouble since Eve began it.
In Africa and Asia, in Albion and Spain,
Trouble and sorrow and wars and pain—
Never any quietude, never any peace
In Italy or Egypt or Palestine or Greece.
Half the world in turmoil, with woe bent double!
Yet you must go discovering a brand-new trouble."

The winds from the spheres grew shrill and loud.
　　Now shivered the saints anointed.
Christopher Columbus knelt upon a cloud
　　And looked where the Master pointed.
"Sailor," said the Lord, "four hundred years
This land has been a crying, a clamor in My ears,
While you lay sleeping till the Judgment Day.
Now rise and answer for the U.S.A."

From the golden pavement, from the gateway pearled,
Columbus looked on the spinning world.
He saw the mountains, and he saw the sea,
He saw America where India should be.
He saw the cities and the fields of grain,
And he heard the voice of the Lord complain:

"Behold the things that you brought to pass:
The great towns bellowing in tones of brass;
Billboards rising where the wild deer wandered,
The earth despoiled and the forests squandered;
Men looking down where My hills used to look up;
Swing bands squealing on a national hookup;
Strikes and riots
　　And bursting dams;

Hollywood diets
   And subway jams;
A thousand new religions shouting out their wares;
Floods and dust bowls and two World Fairs;
Politics and panics and boys in breadlines,
And everywhere the sound of their shrieking headlines.
The heroes dead and the giants departed.
Now rise and answer for the thing you started!"

Christopher Columbus, sturdy old tar,
Stood up straight at the Judgment Bar.
He bowed to Michael with his shining sword,
   He bowed to the Great White Throne.
Then Christopher Columbus spoke to the Lord
   In a reasonable tone:

"I saw the mountains, I saw the plain,
I saw the place where my ships had lain,
And reaching northward till time took flight,
There was America, gleaming in the light.
I heard the tumult, I heard the clamor,
The hiss of the rivet, the noise of the hammer,
The speeches and the shouting and the sound of cheers
And, Lord, it was strange to my sleep-filled ears.
But I saw such wonders and I heard such mirth
As I never knew when I walked on earth!

"A proud young race and their children and their sires,
Dwelling in their houses, working at their fires;
And some were weeping,
   And some were old,
And some were sleeping,
   Hungry and cold,
And some were wailing for the times askew,
But, Lord, it was better than the world I knew.

"Tanned and tall were their sons and their daughters.
They had won the valleys, they had tamed the waters.

I saw them soaring
   Through the conquered air.
Their trains went roaring
   Everywhere.
Strong their buildings and their bridges stood.
The land was fertile and the harvests good.
And a hundred million people
   Lived in brotherhood.
The Jew and the Gentile had joined their labor.
And none there feared to address his neighbor.
And there was order
   And the guns had died
Along their border,
   A continent wide.

"And freedom still on their hilltops hovered.
Lord, I have seen what my ships discovered.
Let whirlwind shake it, let lightning strike it.
I have looked on this land, and, Lord, I like it."

In the Golden City there was silence for a while.
Then the watching angels saw Jehovah smile.
And He chuckled, "There's sense in a sailor lad.
It's a noisy nation, but it's not so bad.
You rose in heaven
   And you had your say.
And you are forgiven
   For the U.S.A."

Oh, there was rejoicing on the utmost star
When Columbus came from the Judgment Bar.

Millennium

Someday,
Some blank, odd, pallid, immemorial day,
Some curious Monday,
Some Tuesday, Wednesday, Thursday, Friday, Saturday,
Or even Sunday,
I shall arise disheveled and a gaper,
To scan the paper
And stare thereon, thumb through, search it for clues,
Peruse and re-peruse,
And find no news.

Nothing to heat the blood or race the pulse,
Nothing at all—
No six-inch headlines screaming a war's results
Or a city's fall.
No threats, no bombs, no air-raids, no alarms,
No feats of arms,
No foe at any gate,
No politics, no shouting candidate;
Nothing exclusive, not a censored phrase,
No scoops, no Exposés;
No crisis either foreign or domestic,
Nothing wild, urgent, imminent, or drastic
Happening on the earth.

Only reports of weather and the birth
Of triplets to a lioness at the Zoo,
(Printed within a box)
And yesterday's sermons seeming scarcely new
And something about the White-or-Sundry-Sox;
An actress married or divorced or dead,
Who led
The golfing in some tournament or other.

Oh, I shall smother
In ennui, I shall nod and yawn
And fling the dull sheets upon the lawn,
Bored near to death by what they have to say
On that strange, beautiful day.

In Praise of Diversity

Since this ingenious earth began
    To shape itself from fire and rubble;
Since God invented man, and man
    At once fell to, inventing trouble,
One virtue, one subversive grace
Has chiefly vexed the human race.

One whimsical beatitude,
    Concocted for his gain and glory,
Has man most stoutly misconstrued
    Of all the primal category—
Counting no blessing, but a flaw,
That Difference is the mortal law.

Adam, perhaps, while toiling late,
    With life a book still strange to read in,
Saw his new world, how variegate,
    And mourned, "It was not so in Eden,"
Confusing thus from the beginning
Unlikeness with original sinning.

And still the sons of Adam's clay
    Labor in person or by proxy

291

At altering to a common way
   The planet's holy heterodoxy.
Till now, so dogged is the breed,
Almost it seems that they succeed.

One shrill, monotonous, level note
   The human orchestra's reduced to.
Man casts his ballot, turns his coat,
   Gets born, gets buried as he used to,
Makes war, makes love—but with a kind
Of masked and universal mind.

His good has no naunces. He
   Doubts or believes with total passion.
Heretics choose for heresy
   Whatever's the prevailing fashion.
Those wearing Tolerance for a label
Call other views intolerable.

"For or Against" 's the only rule.
   Damned are the unconvinced, the floaters.
Now all must go to public school,
   March with the League of Women Voters,
Or else for safety get allied
With a unanimous Other Side.

There's white, there's black; no tint between.
   Truth is a plane that was a prism.
All's Blanshard that's not Bishop Sheen.
   All's treason that's not patriotism.
Faith, charity, hope—now all must fit
One pattern or its opposite.

Or so it seems. Yet who would dare
   Deny that nature planned it other,
When every freckled thrush can wear
   A dapple various from his brother,
When each pale snowflake in the storm
Is false to some imagined norm?

Recalling then what surely was
    The earliest bounty of Creation:
That not a blade among the grass
    But flaunts its difference with elation,
Let us devoutly take no blame
If similar does not mean the same.

And grateful for the wit to see
    Prospects through doors we cannot enter,
Ah! let us praise Diversity
    Which holds the world upon its center.
Praise *con amor'* or *furioso*
The large, the little, and the soso.

Rejoice that under cloud and star
    The planet's more than Maine or Texas.
Bless the delightful fact there are
    Twelve months, nine muses, and two sexes;
And infinite in earth's dominions
Arts, climates, wonders, and opinions.

Praise ice and ember, sand and rock,
    Tiger and dove and ends and sources;
Space travelers, and who only walk
    Like mailmen round familiar courses;
Praise vintage grapes and tavern Grappas,
And bankers and Phi Beta Kappas;

Each in its moment justified,
    Praise knowledge, theory, second guesses;
That which must wither or abide;
    Prim men, and men like wildernesses;
And men of peace and men of mayhem
And pipers and the ones who pay 'em.

Praise the disheveled, praise the sleek;
    Austerity and hearts-and-flowers;

People who turn the other cheek
    And extroverts who take cold showers;
Saints we can name a holy day for
And infidels the saints can pray for.

Praise youth for pulling things apart,
    Toppling the idols, breaking leases;
Then from the upset apple-cart
    Praise oldsters picking up the pieces.
Praise wisdom, hard to be a friend to,
And folly one can condescend to.

Praise what conforms and what is odd,
    Remembering, if the weather worsens
Along the way, that even God
    Is said to be three separate Persons.
Then upright or upon the knee,
Praise Him that by His courtesy,
For all our prejudice and pains,
Diverse His Creature still remains.

INDEX OF TITLES AND
FIRST LINES

297